BALEARIC ISLANDS

NAGEL'S
ENCYCLOPEDIA-GUIDE

GOLD MEDAL OF THE CITY OF ROME
GREAT SILVER MEDAL, PARIS

THE BALEARIC ISLANDS

128 pages
3 black-and-white plans
3 maps in colour

Second revised edition

NAGEL PUBLISHERS
GENEVA PARIS MUNICH

Edited by M. Jacques HEERS, former professor at the University of Algiers

First edition, 1962
Second edition, 1969

ISBN 2–8263–0306–6

© 1975 by Nagel Publishers, Geneva (Switzerland)
All rights reserved in all countries, including the U.S.S.R.
Printed in Switzerland

CONTENTS

Publisher's Note 7; Geography 10; History 11; Local traditions 18.

Majorca The countryside	21
Palma	29
I. The Cathedral district	31
II. The district of palaces and churches	35
III. The northern districts........................	39
IV. The Lonja and the eastern districts	43
Excursions round Palma	47
I. The western beaches and the suburbs	47
II. Bellver Castle, Genova and Son Roca	48
III. The east coast	51
Excursions in the island of Majorca	53
I. The Sierra Burguesa	53
II. Andraitx and the south-west coast...............	54
III. Valldemosa, Soller and the north coast	56
IV. Pollensa, Formentor and the north-east	62
V. Manacor and the caves of the east coast	68
VI. Lluchmayor, Santañy and the south-east	73
Minorca The countryside	77
Mahon	78
Excursions in the surroundings of Mahon	82
Ciudadela	83
The road from Mahon to Ciudadela	85

CONTENTS

Ibiza   Its originality 87
  Ibiza-Town 90
  Excursions in the island........................... 93
Practical information 95
Spanish dictionary 111
Index.. 119

MAPS AND PLANS in colour:

Balearic Islands 8-9
Plan of Majorca 24-25
Plan of Palma 40-41

in black and white

The surroundings of Palma........................... 49
Minorca 79
Ibiza 89

PUBLISHER'S NOTE

The *Balearic Islands* have become one of the most sought after spots in European tourism. The attraction of their splendid countryside, the architectural beauty of their buildings, the hospitality of their inhabitants, all combine to make a visit to these new "fortunate islands" full of enchantment. The increased facility of sea and air communications has enhanced their tourist prestige which their mild climate—pleasant at all times of year—justifies still further.

Thus we felt it was essential that we should add a guide on the Balearic Islands to our list. Although it is naturally a slim volume, it nonetheless is as complete as possible. We owe its scholarly style to the erudition of our collaborator, M. *Jacques Heers*, former professor at Algiers University, and specialist on the Mediterranean countries, and we should like to thank him herewith.

We hope to be of help to all tourists who visit the Balearic Islands, and we should be most grateful for any suggestions they might like to make.

PUBLISHER'S NOTE
2nd edition

The rapid strides made in tourism in the Balearic Islands reflect the attraction of these enchanting islands for the tourist. Since many new developments have occurred as a result of this growth in the tourist industry, a new carefully revised and up-dated version of this guide was called for. Thus the present Encyclopedia-Guide, which incorporates the most recent developments, will be all the more useful. Like all other titles in this collection, "The Balearic Islands" contains no adversising of any kind and all information presented is entirely objective.

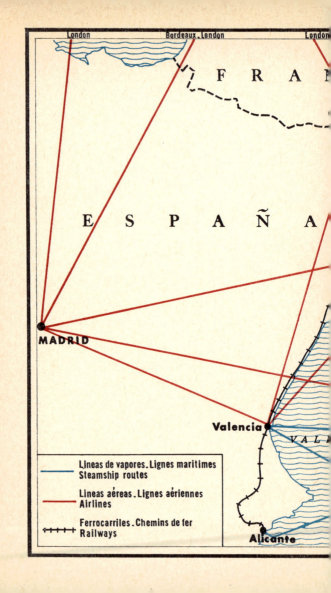

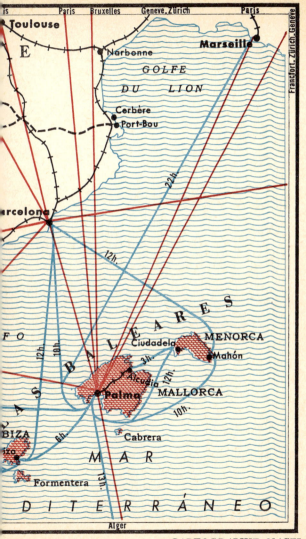

CARTOGRAPHIE NAGEL

GEOGRAPHY

The **climate** of the Balearic Islands is one of the most pleasant in the Mediterranean zone. In summer, the sea breeze and sometimes the altitude keep the temperature from becoming uncomfortably hot. The winter is uniformly mild, especially in Majorca; the average temperature at Palma is above 57.2° F and frost is practically unknown. Showers are quickly followed by a return of the brilliant sunlight.

The variety of the *countryside* often surprises the visitor to the islands; it will be described below, preceding the section devoted to each island. Here we might just mention that Majorca and Minorca in the north and Ibiza and Formentera to the south belong to different worlds and – apart from their Mediterranean features – have little in common. This variety, this quality of surprise, make up much of their charm and attraction to the traveller.

At 175 km from the Spanish coast, *Majorca* is a mountainous island; there we find the limestone "sierras" stretching along the skyline to the north-east, continuations of the Andalusian and eastern Spanish mountain ranges. The northern range is particularly imposing: it reaches a height of 4,740 feet at the Puig Mayor and its sheer, craggy white rocks often tower more than 3,280 feet above the sea. A wide depression separates it from another "sierra", with more moderate rounded peaks. The *Pityusae* also have hilly parts.

In contrast, *Minorca* is formed entirely of a huge, even limestone plateau which shows only a few traces of former heights in the north. It is wide open to the north winds, offering little shelter, and has no means of irrigation: thus it is a dry, monotonous country, an island of cattle with vast pasture lands. Majorca, on the other hand, is the "island of trees"; olive trees on the slopes, almond trees in the plains, orange trees in the irrigated "huertas" at the back of the valleys; a smiling landscape whose changing verdure stands in contrast to the bareness of Minorca.

HISTORY

The differences which divide one island from the other, sometimes one district from the other, have been accentuated by the inhabitants themselves. They came from every corner of the Mediterranean world and brought their own culture with them; by their hard work they shaped the landscape into the pattern familiar to them. A true crossroads of the Mediterranean, the Balearic Islands have been subject to every conceivable influence: Eastern, African, Spanish Christian; but they often modified them, remaining a world apart.

ANTIQUITY

The islands have a long Eastern and Greek history. The oldest traces are found in the huge walls and defence towers, also the Minorcan tombs which are reminiscent of the Sardinian "nuraghe" and were doubtlessly built by a kindred people. The Greeks did not establish strong colonies here as they did in Sicily; the only traces they have left are some clay and bronze figurines. From the middle of the 7th century B.C. Carthage founded Ibiza as a citadel and base for the fleet on the route to Spain. Its influence is evident to this day in the local traditions (music and costumes) and in the peasant houses which have a very individual character. The southern islands, the Pityusae, have thus retained an Oriental character.

The Romans took Majorca in 121 B.C. But, from what has so far been gleaned from archaeological research work, their occupation appears to have been very superficial; doubtlessly they regarded Majorca simply as a stepping stone in their maritime lines of communication. The Balearic Islands, like many other Mediterranean islands, were not deeply marked by Rome and the Empire. Monuments of that period are rare; only the theatre of Pollentia near the bay of Alcudia—where the ships used to anchor—deserves some attention.

After the collapse of the *pax Romana*, the Balearic Islands experienced almost a century of Vandal occupation. Then, in

533, they were conquered by the Byzantine armies of Belisarius; the islands were governed by Greek officials; they again became military bases and maintained active trading connexions with Constantinople. During the "barbarian period", the Balearic Islands thus lived somewhat apart from the Iberian peninsula which, dominated by its own monarchy (that of the Visigoths) and its all-powerful church, was already taking shape as Spain round the authority of its bishops. This special position at a time when the Continental provinces were beginning to be aware of a national concept doubtlessly explains many of the original characteristics of the islands.

ISLAM AND THE CHRISTIAN RECONQUEST

The Arab invasion was very swift. After conquering the Visigoths in 711, the Moors occupied the islands a few years later and confirmed their domination by a series of impressive military buildings; thus there rose the Arab castle near Pollensa, *Castell del Rey* and the imposing ramparts of Alcudia. Yet, Arab influence on the islands was perhaps less strong than in other Mediterranean regions; at least, their civilization there was essentially rural. Although there are still Moorish baths in Palma, dating from the 10th century, which suggest a sophisticated urban life, and although the chroniclers sometimes speak admiringly of Alcudia which was then the capital, it is certain that the Arabs did not give the Balearic Islands a single city that could rival those of Andalusia. The islands were inhabited by officials, soldiers and peasants. It is in country things (the type of house found in Majorca, embroidery designs, pottery techniques and motifs, wrought-iron work) that the surest traces of Arab influence in the Balearic Islands are to be found. The density of the Moorish population in the countryside throughout the centuries of Moslem domination is borne out by the number of large villages or hamlets that still retain names of Arab origin (names ending in –*bini*, especially in Majorca).

The Arab occupation, though limited, continued for five centuries. When all the other western Mediterranean islands had already been recaptured (Corsica, Sardinia, Sicily) and the reconquest of the Peninsula was well under way, when the Crusaders had long been established in the Holy Land, the Balearic Islands still remained Moslem territory and a refuge of pirates, in the heart of a Christian sea. It was mainly the wish to put down piracy that prompted the expedition of the King of Aragon at the beginning of the 13th century. In September 1229

Jaime (James) I blockaded the town of Majorca at the head of a vast fleet of Catalan and Italian ships; the army landed in an adjacent bay and, during the winter, took the town; but the conquest of the islands was difficult (Minorca 1232, Ibiza 1235). When it succeeded it made a great stir in the West, corresponding to the victory of Navas de Tolosa a few years previously (1212) which opened the way to the Andalusian towns for the King of Castile.

Jaime I founded the **Kingdom of Majorca,** a sovereign and independent state, based on the two capitals of Perpignan and Majorca, the first traditional, feudal and land-minded, the latter new, "colonial", its interests centred on the sea. At first these territories, which had so lately been brought back to a Christian way of life, presented the same problems which Christian knights and princes had experienced in the peninsula and the Holy Land. Thus the islands passed through a rather difficult period, the period of reconquest and colonization.

The first problem was that of repeopling the land: Majorca, fertile and well cultivated, could receive a large number of peasants. So the king distributed among his followers—fortuneless knights in search of a more fruitful career—domains scattered throughout the whole island. These *repartimientos* complicated the population problem still further since they did not come from the same regions: among them were Aragonese, Catalans, bringing with them their own skills, their own ways of building houses or of working the land; they often created a series of disjointed "countries" in the islands, each with its individual character. But we must remember that not all lands were thus distributed and that the Moslem population, more or less converted, often stayed put, and in many places continued to work their fields.

Traces of the military aspects of the reconquest still remain. Usually the kings of Majorca contented themselves with rebuilding the old Moorish strongholds which had been dismantled during the fighting; this happened in the case of the *Castell del Rey* overlooking the bay of Pollensa and the towers of the *Palace of Palms*, erected on the ruins of the Almudaina, the Arab fortress; on the outskirts, the castle of *Bellver* shows the influence of Perpignan art. The religious conquest was in the hands of the regular orders—as everywhere in "colonial" lands—and especially in those of the Mendicant Friars; their activity was mostly limited to the large towns where the Dominicans and Franciscans had their monasteries. But the very symbol of the reconquest—religious and military—is the Cathedral of Palma which—facing the bay—dwarfs the countryside with its imposing and austere bulk. It is a church whose magnificent upward drive expresses all the spiritual qualities of Gothic art but shows also the military preoccupations of the period; its serried ranks of solid buttresses seem ready to defy all assaults.

THE GOLDEN AGE (13th—15th century)

In 1343, after a bitter struggle, the kingdom of Majorca lost its independence and was finally joined again to the kingdom of Aragon during the reign of Pedro IV. This union marked the end of the heroic and difficult era of the Reconquest for the Balearic Islands; it heralded the golden age of Majorca. For about two centuries—the 14th and 15th—the island enjoyed a period of exceptional commercial prosperity; this was the great age of its history, which brought it money and a taste for the arts, which gave it a distinguished aristocracy and its strong personality. The King of Aragon had successfully extended his influence over most of the shores of the Western Mediterranean; he had founded a real empire of the sea, and Majorca was one of its loveliest ornaments—and one of the most useful. Situated at the crossing of the great trade routes, the island became the obligatory port of call in the West.

The people, however, were peasants rather than sailors. They had little wood for building ships and had to content themselves with Ibiza pines for their special single-masted boats or have timber brought from the Catalan coast, from the Monseny forests. The Balearic Islands had no great fleet comparable to those of the Italian maritime republics, Pisa, Genoa or Venice; but they had hardy and enterprising sailors who were the first, at the end of the 13th century, to organize voyages to the North Sea from the Mediterranean by the Straits of Gibraltar. The best school of cartography in the West grew up there, and its portulans were sought after; this school received German and Genoese scholars (Martin Behaim) in the 15th century and played an essential part in the preparation of the great journeys of discovery. There is no doubt that Christopher Columbus owes much of his success to Majorca.

But it was mainly foreign ships that assured the fortune of the island, which had become the port of call on all major routes. The Catalans of Barcelona, Perpignan, and Collioure made it a warehouse for their African and Oriental trade. The Italian fleets which had helped to recapture the town—paid by Jaime I—in the

13th century continued to visit the port. Numerous Pisans, Genoese, Venetians and Florentines came there, in ships laden with all the wealth of Asia, bringing their capital and their bold initiative. An international centre, Majorca experienced a brilliant era, illustrated by the *Lonja of the Sea* near the harbour; this is a splendid building, in reality an Exchange where contracts were sealed and rates of exchange fixed. It was erected for the merchants, and bears witnesses to a stable civilization, dominated by merchants and seafarers.

This activity was, of course, confined to the capital and its harbour. Elsewhere the coast was hostile, and little visited; it had to be defended against pirates. The Majorcans built watchtowers and fortified castles on the mountainous spurs. Towns avoided the coast, as everywhere along the Mediterranean shores which were too exposed to attacks from the sea. Thus they are double villages: on one hand we have the borough, the fortified refuge with tall houses closely hugging the narrow little streets, with ramparts built above the lonely countryside, with walls whose high windows were difficult to reach; yet, these perching villages were less austere, less exclusively "military" than thoses of Provence, of Liguria or Calabria. On the other hand, a few fishermen's houses by the seashore, along a quay—often a rudimentary one—formed the *puerto*. Several kilometres separated the two centres which yet depended on one another—e. g. at Soller, Pollensa or Felanitx. The island exported only few products and—apart from Palma which lived mainly on *entrepot* and transit trade—maritime life did not amount to very much, in spite of coral fishing.

There was a strong contrast between Majorca and its neighbours: whereas a brilliant urban civilization developed at Palma, Minorca remained outside the main stream of trade; it only exported its wool which its light ships carried to Majorca. Ibiza was simply the island of salt, exploited by banking companies from Catalonia or Italy.

This was the happy era that brought riches to Palma—which was still called the "city of Majorca" *(Ciudad de Mallorca)* until, it seems, the beginning of the 16th century. Ships arrived from all parts of the known world. But its history and its position made Palma especially a port of call on the routes from Africa, a kind of meeting place between the Christian and the Moslem worlds. The bulk of trade was with Tunis, Bougie, and the great coral fisheries of La Calle, Algiers, Oran and Tlemcen; corn was brought from Africa, wax, honey, leather and the products from the caravans in the Sahara; gum-arabic, ostrich feathers, gold from the Sudan, all that was richest and most desirable. The memory of past splendour still hangs over Palma like an exotic perfume.

One man symbolizes the strange position of the island towards Islam. That is Raymond Lull whom the Majorcans still admire deeply. A great traveller, monk, scholar, with a perfect knowledge of the doctrines of Christianity and of Islam, for a time professor at Paris, he was one of the rare preachers of his time who took an interest in the Moslem world; he travelled through it many times as far as the Orient, in a courageous and stubborn effort to achieve conversions. Several times made prisoner, he finally was stoned to death by the Arabs in North Africa in 1314. His life story soon became embroidered with legend, so much did his unusual career fire the imagination. For a long time after him Majorca remained the centre of Christianity which took the greatest interest in the Orient and Africa.

THE AGE OF THE NOBILITY (16th–18th century)

In 1469 under Ferdinand of Aragon and Isabella of Castile the Balearic Islands became part of the Kingdom of Spain. This marked the beginning of a gilded decadence in the islands. Very soon Spain was to turn towards the Atlantic with brilliant success; the Balearic Islands remained outside the country's activities; they did not benefit from the riches which colonial trade brought to the cities of Andalusia or the Basque country. At the beginning of the 16th century, when foreign gold ceased to flow into the port, Majorca underwent an economic crisis. It was a difficult period, with popular upheavals the most serious of which—the rising of the *germanios* (artisans) in 1521—forced the surviving nobles to flee to Ibiza and to remain in exile for more than two years. It was also an insecure period in which the island had to fight the Berber pirates who were constantly harassing the coast from Algiers. New fortresses were built to defend it: Charles V had imposing walls built round Ibiza, but Mahon was twice pillaged and sacked.

Majorca ceased to be a port open to the outer world and began to be absorbed in its own affairs, very quietly; Palma's trade declined. Only Dutch shops still came to Ibiza to take on salt. The nobles, less enterprising now, began to grow more conscious of their wealth; there was more leisure for them, and more ambition to demonstrate their success. The 16th and 17th centuries were the age when landscape came to be appreciated, the return to the land. It was—as at Venice—an era of palaces and great villas, of woodwork and fine furniture. Life had changed considerably for the great nobles: there was less grandeur, perhaps, but more comfort. They built their section of the city of Palma—the part which now is the cathedral district—and the residential mansions of the Majorcan countryside.

The sumptuous residences of the nobility have an undefinable charm and stateliness. Modest from the outside, they lead through an entrance into a sombre and mysterious patio: this is a narrow courtyard, very different from the bright, flower-filled Andalusian patio. A formal staircase leads to the first floor where a loggia with wrought-iron railings rests on flattened arches and massive, coarse pillars. In the 18th century another style began to assert itself with the baroque, both architecturally and as a way of life, and triumphed in Palma as it did at Naples, in Sicily, Genoa or Venice. Brighter windows opened along the whole façade; the wider patio took on a regular shape, and was decorated with stone balustrades and delicate pillars with finely worked capitals; the lines of the staircase became less rigid, lighter. But Majorcan baroque retained sobriety—and even a certain austerity—in the façade; here we find few great balconies; in Palma we are a long way from the somewhat vulgar exuberance of Valencia where the windows, set in a stucco decor worthy of goldsmiths' work, are supported by giant caryatides; there are very few examples of this in the Balearic Islands.

The luxury is wholly confined to the interior: rich ornate ceilings ("artesonados" ceilings), brocade tapestries and hangings, valuable furniture; houses that were like museums where one could be at home, secluded, away from the common crowd. The same way of life could also be found in the country, but there it was more open, gayer. Each noble family had its country mansion, called *quinta* (or *finca*). Their country houses had painted façades, in the Italian manner, flowered patios and artistically laid-out gardens; an example may be found at Son Torella near the township of Santa Maria.

The baroque churches doubtlessly show a light spirit and a love of colour, but they also retain, more than in Spain, some form of Gothic and of its moderation. There are very few ornate façades; the naves do not crumble beneath the weight of gilt and stucco—perhaps gold was scarce there whereas there was plenty in Castile and Andalusia; we have to look for showy displays, for coloured frescoes, in the chapels or apses.

In the 18th century the islands did not all share the same fate. Minorca had a troubled period; the Spaniards had to contend for it with the English who wanted to use the famous roadstead of Mahon with its natural defences as a mighty naval base, on the model of Gibraltar. They took it at the beginning of the 18th century and held it until 1756; driven out by the French fleet in that year, they returned to the island in 1763 by the terms of the Treaty of Paris which acknowledged their naval and colonial supremacy there. Forced to leave Majorca again in 1782, they were to occupy it again on two occasions, although only for short periods, 1798–1802 and 1805–1808. The English occupation left few noticeable traces on the island, except for some houses—whose sash windows are rather an oddity—in the towns of Mahon and Ciudadela.

LOCAL TRADITIONS

The traditions of the Balearic Islands are as varied as the origins or their inhabitants. We find here every possible Mediterranean influence: Moorish, sometimes Jewish, chiefly Catalan; all this against a background of a very old Oriental culture and traditions. It is doubtlessly the latter which are the cause of the country's great originality; they are found especially in the south, in the strange houses of the island of Ibiza and in the superb ceremonial costumes of the women. The costumes of the Majorcan women—seen mostly at performances of local dances—are simpler, a sort of large black embroidered headdress and brightly-coloured aprons.

Music played an important part in the daily life of the countryside; here we find a rich tradition, as in Corsica or Sardinia, often showing Arab influences, of a very simple, almost primitive, nature. But now we rarely hear these old melodies which the peasants used to sing as they worked their fields. The dances are easier to learn and to understand; they have been encouraged by travellers who always like seeing them. In Majorca a number of societies (e.g. that of "Pont d'Inca") endeavour to keep them alive or to revive them. These dances are very varied, but almost always very lively: the *jota* brought by immigrants from Aragon, the slower *bolero* or *parado* and the more popular *mateixas* especially used for peasant festivals; thus the *mateixas des figuras*, for instance, mimicks the picking of figs.

The popular festivals may not have the exuberance of those of Castile or Andalusia; but Christmas, Epiphany and Holy Week are celebrated in Palma with all manner of festivities and processions through the illuminated city. The most famous festivals in the island are those of Pollensa in honour of Saint Anthony and Saint Sebastian in January, with a dance of cardboard horses, and the processions of Easter and Corpus Christi.

LOCAL TRADITIONS

Majorca has preserved its ancient crafts and its shops offer —besides the inevitable rubbish for the hurried tourist—well-made and tasteful goods. Popular art has survived here, with its simplicity, its somewhat rough look, its country humour. First of all, ceramics—the old and famous *maiolica*—known since the Middle Ages. Now we find chiefly ceramic tiles of all sizes, to be hung on walls, in a setting of finely-worked wrought iron. They show pictures of work in the fields, drawn with an intimate verve, or illustrate old sayings and proverbs; others form a series, the most widespread being of course the life of Don Quixote, an inexhaustible theme which was taken up by the Spanish craftsmen in the 17th century and transmitted by them as far as to Latin America. Glass goods also have achieved a certain fame and show much originality; shaped bottles and flasks, yellow or smoked glass lanterns, vases and glass goblets painted with colourful flowers. There are also some fine wrought-iron goods: candlesticks, stands, etc. with their complex arabesques or their strangely stylised animals.

Majorca tiles may no longer be easy to obtain, but tourism has given a fresh impetus to embroidery. Table linen with red and blue flowers and a wealth of designs, retains an Oriental style and reminds us of Turkish embroidery or Persian miniatures. But before leaving Palma, we must not omit to look at the very opposite of this delicate art-form, at the strange terra-cotta toys, coarsely painted in white, with red and green stripes.

MAJORCA

THE COUNTRYSIDE

The island of Majorca is the largest of the Balearic Islands with a surface of 3,640 square km; its greatest length E to W is 100 km, its width N to S 75 km. It has about 360,000 inhabitants. Its relief is rather contorted; three natural regions, from S-W to N-E are a continuation of the geographic features of the peninsula. This complexity of its natural features make Majorca a most varied country in its landscapes, ways of life and agricultural produce.

THE NORTHERN SIERRA

If we arrive from Barcelona or Paris by plane, we see the Northern Sierra with dramatic suddenness, a very prominent limestone barrier. It is a tangle of jagged ridges, rough peaks and shut-in ravines. There are massive ranges such as the Puig Mayor range which reaches an altitude of 4,740 feet near Soller, but also jagged ridges, strange landscapes of large limestone slabs broken through by erosion, split by wide crevices. The most striking part of this landscape is found round Lluch. The Sierra rises in steep white rocks above the sea, dressed with clumps of pines and sometimes with villages closely hugging their scraggy peak.

This is one of the most picturesque coasts of the western Mediterranean: a "costa brava" which can hold its own with that of Catalonia. It overlooks the sea from high cliffs of changing hues, is sometimes straight, but more often cut up into long, rugged headlands with strange shapes which are thrust out far into the waves. The most extraordinary of these is the Cape of Formentor, at the N-E end of the island, with its grey or red walls, its large pinewoods and its lovely sandy beach. Along the shore the mountain streams, which are almost invariably dry in summer, end in deep gorges between sheer rocks; these are the wooded "calanques" (inlets) with their shingle beaches washed by a calm and transparent sea—that of the Torrent of Pareys, the Cala de San Vincente. In other parts, tiny rounded bays —especially that of Puerto de Soller whose curve is almost unbelievably perfect—shelter at the foot of high headlands, dominated by old watchtowers.

In the whole of this northern mountain region communications are naturally difficult; the passes can only be reached by long, winding roads going through an arid countryside. Here we see the Mediterranean mountain country *par excellence*, very much partitioned, with isolated cantons, with its pockets of cultivated land, each with its own way of life. This region does not live entirely on picturesqueness and tourism. Natural conditions favour shrub growing and the careful cultivation of fields and vineyards. The Sierra protects the country from the often formidable north winds, and Majorca, the "Isla Blanca" is also the "Isla Calma". Numerous sources fed by rain and the snow from the peaks supply the necessary water. Although the heights are given over to pinewoods, bent by the winds, or to a poor *maquis* (heath) scented by myrtle or rosemary or even shrubs of dwarf palms, all the slopes and valleys are cultivated.

The conquest of the Sierra has cost the Majorcan peasant a great effort; the steepest slopes are cut up into minute terraces of some few square yards which form huge stairways down to the rio or the sea. They are supported by immense walls of dry stones which are constantly in danger from water and landslides, but which are always rebuilt; these terraces everywhere are the determining feature of the landscape. The northern region is above all the land of the olive tree, of oil, where each farm had its own press. All the terraces along the slopes are taken up by olive trees; very old trees, showing a long tradition of farming. Sometimes there are fig trees among them, and more and more frequently now the carob-tree. The red soil beneath the great olive trees with their light foliage is sown each year and produces some cereals or vegetables. In more open and level parts, near Pollensa for instance, the soil is manured with ashes of holm-oak or olive branches which are burnt slowly on the spot, and barley, oats or wheat are grown on it.

More fragile and difficult crops are grown lower down; this is the region of the irrigated *huertas* where each square inch of land is the object of tender care. These huertas, near Soller, Pollensa and Deya, are shut in at the back of valleys, fed directly by stream water by means of a host of little canals which are strictly controlled by the peasant community. Here the main crops are oranges, lemons and medlars, grown in tiny enclosures where some early vegetables are also planted. Some of the higher huertas, at Banalbufar or Estellenchs have their fields along the slopes; the terraces are irrigated by source water which is first collected in vast basins hollowed out of the rock, then distributed by small cemented channels—the "seguias"—on the model of those in the mountains of North Africa; here there are fewer trees but more vegetables.

THE PLAIN

In the centre of the island, at the foot of the Sierra, lies the large plain of Majorca, a huge hollow surrounded by mountains. It has two wide openings to the sea, the bay of Palma at the S-W end and that of Alcudia at the N-E end, so that communications are easy. Here the two capitals of the island established themselves in turn: the Roman *Pollentia* which later became the Moorish Alcudia, and Catalan and Christian Palma. The Majorcan plain, rather unusual in this rugged country, does not give the impression of monotony; not only are the northern mountains constantly in view, but there are also occasional rounded hillocks, of a modest height it is true (330 to 700 feet), with villages whose belfry and castle dominate the plain. This region has no true peasantry nor homesteads isolated in the midst of fields. The population here is urban, living together in large boroughs which they have to leave very early every morning to get to their fields. Along the little country roads at that time, and also late in the evening, we may see a long procession of men and women with their mules and their donkeys, sometimes a two-wheeled cart which —on feast days— is richly decorated with flowers.

The chief problem of the limestone plain—sheltered, as it is, from the damp winds— is that of water, since there are no sources. Rain water is collected in large cisterns near the homesteads. The cisterns, made of masonery embedded in the soil, are one of the characteristic features of the central part of Majorca. Each house has one or two, standing well sheltered in the shade. Sometimes water is collected in wells. In either case, it has to be distributed by means of irrigation canals which run along the fields, and it has to be brought up. The oldest way of doing this —a very primitive one—was by bucket-chain, as in the East. In certain parts of Majorca this can still be seen. A mule turns a very simple mechanism, a vertical wheel to which are attached earthen containers which are emptied in turn. But to draw water from a greater depth the force of the wind is used in the little huertas of the valley and in the better irrigated surroundings of

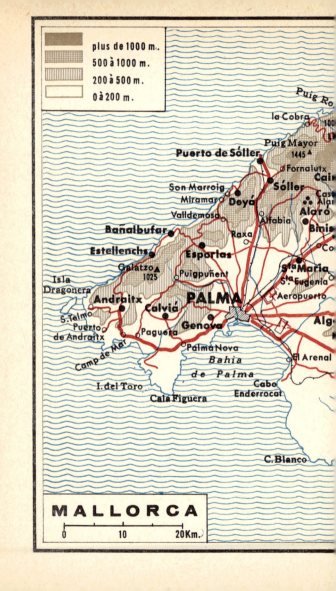

Majorca. Windmills were built—very rustic-looking ones with their wide vanes turning incessantly in the wind; along the roads from Palma to Manacor or to Lluchmayor each house has its own and the whole countryside is alive with the constant rustling of windmills. Elsewhere there are much more complex, proper windmills; they can be seen on every hillock. There are those of Inca, of Santa Catalina at Palma where a whole district is called "El Molinar"; they surround Manacor with a white halo. These mills have their own distinctive style, with their six vanes fixed to an adjustable mast; the sails are controlled by a whole series of roping and can be furled or unfurled to the wind as in a sailing boat.

Cultivation varies considerably according to the water supply and the nature of the soil. Majorca was for a long time a wheat country; some wheat is still being grown beneath the almond trees. But now it only plays a small part in the life of the island. At the foot of the mountains and along the pebbly terraces of the slopes vineyards have been developed, especially at Binisalem which is famous for its white wines with their high alcohol content. Elsewhere there are figs, grown on great, bushy trees. But the main crop of the plain are almonds; introduced recently, the trees are now spreading through whole regions which disappear under their blossoms in February. This has become a considerable source of livelihood for the island people and has given the peasants in the plain a new lease of life. It has become Majorca's main export (almonds in shells, roasted almonds, *dragées*, nougats and all kinds of preserves).

THE SOUTH

The southern part of Majorca consists of another mountain range, but a less rugged one than the northern Sierra. Here the mountains form a series of little mounds, bulky and rounded, without jags, reaching rarely as much as 1640 feet. Often used as defence gates by the monasteries which also had their places of pilgrimage there, the relief here is not very significant. The towns and villages avoid the hills, being rather in the plain. This high plateau is the least favoured part of the island. We find the same irrigation difficulties as in the plain, but with less fertile soil. Fortunately the almond tree—towards Felanitx or Santañy— has transformed the economy of the country which was very much cut off. However, in the valleys another kind of tree is being cultivated, namely the peach tree. But communication with the sea is not easy. For a long time the closeness of the coast was a cause of apprehension because of exposure to Berber pirate attacks. In the north of Majorca, the villages are still fairly near the coast, defended by their natural heights and fortifications; in the south they fled farther inland. Santañy is 5 km. from the coast, Felanitx 15 km., Campos still farther. The whole southern shore is a vast deserted area, a sort of limestone slab, cut up by dells and rivers that are almost invariably dry. We gain the same impression of the east where the straight coastline is edged by high cliffs hollowed by underground waters which have made some fantastic caves with stalactites; beyond, a group of isolated peaks in the hinterland and Manacor, the town of the plain remains at some distance from its port, Porto Cristo.

PALMA

Palma *(Palma de Mallorca)* is the only large town in the island and now has almost 170,000 inhabitants. It stands at the back of a wide bay on a remarkable site, terraced on the foothills and dominated by the imposing cathedral of which we catch sight very soon if we arrive by boat. The former residence of the Moorish kings who were installed in the Almudaina palace, but then often supplanted by Alcudia which was considered the capital, Palma owes its prosperity to the Christian reconquest and the kings of Majorca. For several centuries it was the port of the Balearic islands and one of the great trading centres of the western Mediterranean.

After a long period of decline, Palma has recently experienced a revival thanks to the growth of tourism. The journey to Majorca is traditional for Spaniards and many foreigners visit it too because of its pleasant climate, its picturesque city and the island's beaches. Majorca now receives tourists all through the year; to the winter season has been added a no less brilliant summer season, starting with the Easter holidays. It is really the tourist capital of the island. Besides the harbour and aerodrome, there are many hotels and boarding houses of all categories, and roads enabling visitors to see the villages and countryside, as well as easy communications with Minorca and Ibiza.

Apart from tourism, Palma lives on the produce of the island for it is the main agricultural market. A lively food production industry has grown up; preserves and jams, especially of apricots and figs. It exports fresh vegetables and fruit. Fishing is fairly important (especially along the shore) particularly since the growth of the hotel industry whose needs increase each year. In fact, the growth of tourism and its requirements have—as on the Côte d'Azur—played a large part in the economic revival of the town and the surrounding country: the building industry (new hotels spring up each year and modern houses in the suburbs along the road to Bellver castle), works to facilitate transport of market produce and the local wines, a revival of local craftsmanship and even of the leather industry.

Palma has two main centres of interest. The old town crowded round the cathedral and the former royal palace; a city that is still full of charm with its narrow streets without pavements, its dark little stairways, its old houses with fine, severe façades which cast a restful shade in summer. Nor is it a kind of museum city, because it is usually extremely lively, being also the district of the administrative and business offices, with all kinds of shops, cafés and restaurants. Then there is the modern town, along the SW shore, which has absorbed the old fishing suburbs and the country villas; here we find the new hotels whose brightly lit façades illuminate the country at night for miles. The only part which has remained untouched by these changes is the hillock of Santa Catalina with its strange ruins and old flour mills whose silhouette is characteristic of the suburb. Below is the Terreno with its wide avenues and flowered parks; beyond is San Pedro, Ca's Català and farther still the new bathing resort which is called Palma Nova; they stand amidst pinewoods and near creeks with fishing boats, with isolated hotels, and with wide sandy beaches, far from the busy town.

TOUR OF THE TOWN

The main street is **Paseo Generalisimo,** often called **El Borne;** it is a wide tree-lined avenue with a central terreplein which reminds us of the **Ramblas** of Catalonia, Barcelona, Gerona or Tarragona. This is the street of the large stores, the travel agencies and cinemas. As in all Spanish towns, the Paseo is very lively in the evening, thronged with strollers who spend hours there. The Borne is continued to the north by *San Jaime* Avenue, then by *Via Roma* which form the axis of the business centre.

I. The Cathedral district

At the very bottom of the Borne, with your back to the sea, turn into **Calle del Conquistador** which goes diagonally uphill to the right; then you come, immediately after the Teatro Lirico, to a stairway. At the top, still on the right, is the cathedral square; opposite, the Mirador terrace which overlooks the sea; on the right, the Almudaina palace, on the left the W façade of the cathedral.

The **Almudaina** is the former fortress and residence of the Moorish kings; the building was altered considerably by the kings of Majorca and has lost its original look. It was—in the tradition of Arab palaces—a rather disorderly jumble of residential buildings, separate pavilions, kitchens and offices, all kind of outbuildings, all contained in a huge enclosure. Of this pleasant disorder there remains now only the disconcerting lay-out of the modern buildings and the four squat **towers** with Arab decorations; one of them is surmounted by a bronze angel by **Francisco Campredan,** the kind of weathercock statue which Christian architects loved to put on top of their buildings. However, the Christian era has contributed some very valuable parts to the buildings, especially those by the masters of Perpignan of the peak period of Majorcan art. Just opposite us from the entrance is the **Chapel of Santa Ana** the oldest of the Christian buildings, still in romanesque style; the **loggia,** wide open to the bay, elegant and delicate, but a little pedantic, is late Gothic. The Almudaina now houses a barracks; only a part of it may be visited.

The **cathedral,** an outstanding building, strikes us by its majestic look and the severe harmony of its bulk. It is one of the finest examples of Mediterranean

Gothic art, of its mastery of architectural masses, soberly, without facile effects or superfluous ornaments.

In fact, it is a building of very dissimilar parts whose erection took several centuries of uncertainties and improvised solutions. At first—as in many parts of Andalusia after the reconquest, and particularly at Cordóba the old mosque was converted for Christian worship. It was not very large, as befitted a second-rate Moslem town. The Christian architects added the square belfry, a little heavy, perhaps, and above all the main apse to the east of the building; there the royal chapel was installed. These transformations, although very limited in scope, took many years. The high altar was not consecrated until 1346, more than a century after the capture of the town; then the monumental apse was finished, out of proportion with the nave of the former mosque.

It was only in the second half of the 14th century that the building of a new nave was undertaken, a splendid one on the model of the great Gothic cathedrals of the continent. Catalan master-builders—especially *Guillermo Sagrera* who had worked also on the cathedral of Perpignan and Castel Nuovo at Naples—began to be seen on the Palma building site; Sagrera also was in charge of the buildings for the chapter with their remarkable chapter-house. The erection of these new buildings took more than a century. At the end of the 16th century work was still continuing on one of the portals, and the cathedral was not finally consecrated until 1613.

If we stand in the square, we face the **west façade,** which is the oldest one; it dates from the 15th century, but had to be partly rebuilt in the 19th. Surmounted by a triangular pediment and flanked by two tall, very pointed and ornamented belfries, it has an immense Gothic rose-window on the upper part. The portal dates from 1594 and shows a strong Italian influence. On each side are statues of saints (St John the Evangelist, St Jerome and the Blessed Raymond Lull).

The **south façade** is the most beautiful and the most famous one; with its series of flying-buttresses set on bulky pillars it overlooks the sea. The wall is bare, austere-looking, its only ornament being the **Portal of Mirador**—also known as the **portal of the sea**—one of the finest pieces of Catalan gothic sculpture.

Preceded by a vaulted porch which used to be decorated with statues, it is surmounted by a large triangular gable; the arch of the door itself is very bold, rising more than 50 feet above the ground. The statues date from the end of the 14th and beginning of the 15th century. *Guillermo Sagrera*, another Catalan, *Pedro Morey*, and a Fleming, *Jean de Valenciennes*, worked on the portal.

The most interesting statues are those of the *bends* and of the *piers;* we can recognize the prophets, the angels, Old Testament figures. Nearly all show a northern influence—certainly Flemish, as the importance of trade relations with the North Sea would naturally suggest; some of the figures with their stern looks, their long beards and heavy draperies remind us of the Burgundian school. The *tympanum*—entirely sculpted—is divided into two sections: below, the Last Supper, above God the Father among a group of angels. The Virgin of the *pier*, with the Holy Child, is probably a copy of a 15th-century work which can be seen in the nearby diocesan Museum (see below, p. 35).

The **north façade** is much simpler, dominated by the square tower which was built on the minaret of the original mosque. The *Almoina Doorway* has only one rather rudimentary carving: only the bends have delicate leaf-work.

The plan of **the interior** is extremely sober; a nave and two aisles ending in three octogonal apses; no transept nor ambulatory round the choir. But, seen from the inside, the cathedral impresses us with its huge proportions and the boldness of its conception. The vaults (which rise to 144 feet) are upheld by 14 pillars of very pure lines and great delicacy which create a general impression of lightness. The light enters abundantly through three storeys of side windows and by the rose-windows whose stained glass panes (dating from the 19th century) throw a strange—sometimes cruel—light on the pillars and arcades.

The nave and aisles—very high, light, bold yet perfectly harmonious— represent one of the greatest achievements of the Gothic period; the architects, who were then very much masters of their art and had, at the end of the Middle Ages, a considerably improved technical knowledge, knew how to master space and did not try for any facile effects. The huge perspective of the building is broken only at the point of the choir, the "coro" of great Spanish churches where the canons sat and which, unfortunately, is usually hidden by wrought-iron railings or screens of carved wood. But the nave is perfectly disengaged, not even encumbered by rows of chairs; in Spain it is customary to place the chairs only at the times of services. And, not long ago, the women still came to Mass with a mantilla over their heads and carrying, besides the fan and the rosary, a folding-chair held tightly under their arm.

Note first of all the **choir stalls,** finely carved, in a somewhat pedantic and overloaded Gothic style, the work of the Aragonese *Juan de Salas* (1525–1529). The numerous, and often very interesting sculptures and pictures are in the chapels. Above all, we must spare some time for the **royal chapel** in the main apse; baroque *high altar*, 13th-century *bishop's throne*, and old tapestries; the majolica work round the throne is modern. Right at the back, a little raised up, is the **chapel of the Holy Trinity** with the tombs of Jaime II and Jaime III of Majorca.

The **side chapels,** however, are not uniformly interesting. The most noteworthy are: on the right (south), the *chapel of San Pedro* and the statues of San Juan and San Bruno from the Charterhouse of Valldemosa; on the left (north), the *Corpus Christi Chapel* with a magnificent baroque altar-piece by Jaime Blanquer (early 17th century). On the same side a richly decorated door leads to the Sacristy of the canons (treasury of the sacristy with fine baroque goldsmiths' work and 14th-century Gothic altar-piece); another door, at the back of the *Piedad chapel*, leads to the rooms formerly reserved for the chapter; the former Chapter House with beautiful Gothic vaulting, has the tomb of

Gil Munoz who died as bishop of Majorca in 1447 after having been the Antipope Clement VII; then comes a new chapter house in a completely different style, and finally a kind of cloister.

We leave the cathedral at the far end of the nave (west door) and immediately on the right we see the *Almoina house* which dates from the Gothic era but has been greatly transformed. At the back of the square we come to the **Mirador terrace** from which we have a fine *view* of the sea and the suburbs to the west of the town as far as the Bellver hill. Follow the terrace towards the left, along the side of the cathedral to get to the episcopal palace which houses the **Diocesan Museum:**

items found during excavations of pre-Romanesque and Romanesque buildings, collections of paintings by 14th-and 15th-century Majorcan artists, especially the *diptych of the Holy Face and the Virgin* (14th century) and a masterpiece by *Pedro Nisart:* the altar-piece of St George and the dragon with a background of the city and bay of Palma.

II. The district of palaces and churches

We leave from the Borne and take, going up on the right, Calle del Conquistador which we follow right to the end; turn right into *Calle Victoria*, then left, following the tram as far as *Plaza Cort* where we come to the **Casa Consistorial** (Town Hall) with a façade decorated with a porch roof that juts out into the street and with caryatides and rose-windows (in the interior, the *Municipal Museum:* collection of Roman statues brought from Italy).

At the back of the square on the right, still following the tramlines, we take a small street which leads to *Plaza Santa Eulalia*. The **church** of same name was the first to be built in Palma after the Reconquest; of vast proportions, it has, like the cathedral, a nave and two aisles, very high windows which illuminate the nave, and delicate pillars upholding the vaults; here, too, we gain a powerful impression of simplicity and stateliness. The N and S façades date from the end of the Middle Ages; the W façade and the belfry are of recent origin.

Following along the southern façade of Santa Eulalia we come, at the level of the apse, on the right, to a narrow street where we find at No. 2, on the right, the **Palace of the Marquis de Vivot,** a fine mansion built in the 18th century.

The façade is severe, but the *patio* is very elegant, with thick red marble columns, a formal staircase and, on the first floor, a vast loggia along a whole side of the courtyard; another courtyard was used for tables. The apartments have been turned into a museum installed in the drawing rooms with their richly coloured, Italian-style frescoes.

Continue through Calle Zavella and its continuation to *Plaza Guadrado* where you can see to the apse of the **Church of San Francisco.** The Franciscan monastery was begun in 1281 with the aid of King Jaime I. Finished apparently at the end of the 14th century, the church was partly destroyed by fire in 1580. This explains the baroque additions which are often too abundant and unrestrained; work has recently been undertaken to try and restore the building to its original simplicity.

A square *belfry* with windows detached from the bulk of the building, reminiscent of the Arab minaret; the apse is very original, with bulky buttresses and large supporting arches. The *western façade*—on the opposite side (on Plaza San Francisco)—has a large rose-window and a baroque doorway (end 17th century).

The groundplan of the interior is very simple; a single nave and apse, surrounded by many side chapels set between the buttresses, deeper on the left than on the right (side of the cloister). In one of the chapels (left, beyond the choir) is the *tomb of Raymond Lull* dating from 1448.

A door leads to the **cloister** which is very delightful with its palm trees, its old iron-work well and its flowers under the arcades. It is in the best Gothic tradition, lined on four sides by delicate columns upholding fine, slender capitals; above, the arcades with well-defined pointed arches emphasize the lightness of the whole by means of festoons. There is a lightness and grace such as is rarely found in Franciscan cloisters. Two sides have a first storey; here the galleries have no arcades but solid pillars beneath a rustic porch roof with conspicuous beams.

To the south of Plaza San Francisco, opposite the church, take Calle del Padre Nadal; in *Calle del Sol*, on the left, we come to the *Palace of the Marquis of Palmer*, at No. 17. The façade—still severe, but with Renaissance windows, caryatides and stone mullions—dates from 1556. Calle del Sol ends in *Plaza del Templo*. Here there is an Arab fortress, subsequently occupied by the Templars who built dependencies for their house. Of this whole group of buildings—which used to be impressive—only two bulky towers surmounted by battlements and the Oratory of the Temple have survived; the latter dates from the first years after the reconquest and the Oriental influence is very evident, especially in the interior decoration.

On the right of Plaza del Templo—when you are looking at the building,—Calle del Templo branches off to *Plaza de San Jeronimo*, with the Convento de San Jeronimo, 15th century, but with a Renaissance façade, and the College of La Sapiencia (interior courtyard with two storeys of arcades).

Opposite the Convento is Calle del Seminario; at the end of this street, on the left, is the **Church of Montession,** the prototype of a baroque church in Palma. It was begun by the Jesuits at the end of the 16th century (1571) but the building took many years; the façade and doorway date from the end of the 17th century. The porch is very richly decorated, with the statues of the two great patrons of the Jesuit order: Ignatius Loyola and Francis Xavier, and a statue of the Virgin in a closely worked setting of wide scrolls.

The interior also is richly decorated; the painted ceiling (again St Ignatius), columns and capitals, carved wooden altars with gilt covering, coloured stuccoes, all show a wealth and exuberance of effects. The *altar-piece of the Virgin* had been acquired by the Jesuits; it is one of the masterpieces of 15th-century Majorcan painting and may be seen in one of the side chapels.

Following Calle del Vento along the side of the church, we come to Calle San Alfonso and we turn into it to the left for a few yards; at the back of the first street on the right we come to the *Convent of Santa Clara*, one of the oldest in the island; a graceful, Oriental-looking belfry and Gothic altarpieces. Return to Calle San Alfonso and, a little farther on the left, turn into Calle Serra which leads to the *Moorish Baths* at No. 15, one of the few traces left in Palma of the Moslem domination; only a square hall now remains with very flattened arches upholding an elegant cupola. At the end of Calle Serra: *Casa Forminguera*, another mansion with a fine façade and porch roof; it has given its name to a little street by which we can get to Calle Portella. We go up this towards the right; it is lined with fine palaces with wrought-iron railing balconies and little loggias with pretty little bay-windows.

Almost straight on from here we take Calle Morey which we follow to the right until we come to No. 33, the **Casa Oleza,** one of the finest examples of secular architecture in Majorca; built during the Gothic period, but transformed and enlarged in the 16th century when the Oleza family took it over, it shows a successful juxtaposition of two styles: Gothic and Renaissance.

The *façade* is still medieval looking with broken arches, but Plateresque windows have been added in which the artist has used all the decorative motifs of the 16th century: leaf-work on columns and capitals, elsewhere dolphins and shells. The patio has a stone staircase and an old well; very flattened arches are supported by columns with wide Corinthian capitals; the fine first floor was transformed in the 18th century; it opens on to the patio through a wide *loggia*, decorated with a lovely stone balustrade and fine marble ornaments at the base of the columns; on the keystone of the arch is the family's coat-of-arms in a very elaborate Plateresque escutcheon.

A little farther on the left **Calle Almudaina,** shady and picturesque, is typical of Majorca's old streets with several fine façades of mansions, with very elaborate, Plateresque-style windows, decorated with wrought-iron railing balconies. At No. 8 is the 15th-century *Casa Oleo* noteworthy for its patio with banana trees and especially for its interior staircase and stone ramp; it is a comparatively austere, Gothic building.

Along the continuation of Calle Almudaina we return to Calle de Conquistador and we go down this to the left to get back to the Borne.

III. The northern districts

The old town is rather different. There are narrow streets and palaces from a distant era. But the old districts are intersected by wider and straighter roads with trams and cars. There is a busier life, a more crowded one, particularly towards evening round the food and clothes shops.

Go up the Borne again to its far end and along its continuation, *Calle San Jaime*, a very aristocratic street, lined with town mansions. At No. 21, the town *house of the Marquis of Ferrandell*, with vaulted

---

Key to the plan of Palma:

1 Casa Consistorial 2 Diputación 3 Correos 4 Catedral 5 Palacio Episcopal 6 San Francisco 7 San Miguel 8 Teatro 9 Teatro Lírico 10 Consulado de Mar 11 La Lonja del Mar 12 Estación 13 Almudaina 14 Palacio Vivot 15 Casa Oleza 16 Casa Palmer 17 Santa Eulalia 18 Mercado 19 San Felipe de Neri 20 La Merced 21 Santa Cruz 22 Santa Clara

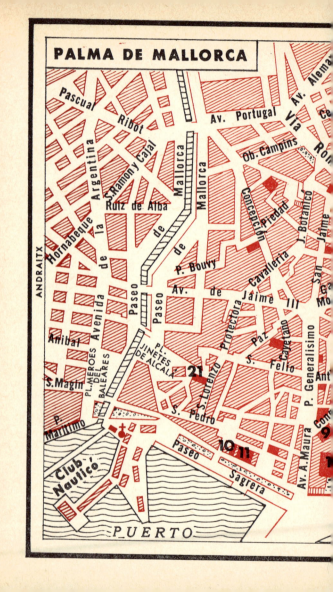

Key to the plan: see over.

entrance, patio and staircase. Farther on, on the right, the *Church of San Jaime,* a 14th-century Gothic church, whose main entrance however is very much later (end 18th century).

Take the road opposite the church, then turn right into *Calle del Jardin Botánico;* at its end, towards the left, begins the *Plaza del Hospital.* Right at the back, in the first courtyard of the present hospital, is the **Santisima Sangre Chapel,** one of the city's most famous buildings. It was built in the second half of the 15th century and has a fine harmony of style, on the classic plan of the Catalonian and Majorcan single-nave churches. This chapel is especially famous for a 14th-century Christ, a polychrome wood statue in southern Gothic style; this is the *Santo Cristo de la Sangre,* much venerated by the people.

On crossing—or following along the north side of— the Botanic Gardens, we can get back to the *Rambla (Via Roma),* a wide street through which the trams run, and we continue down it towards the right. Almost at the very end of the Rambla, take the little *Calle Real* on the left, leading to an old district with shady little streets, towards the **Church of San Miguel.**

In this church, immediately after the reconquest, the city's first Christian service was held in the presence of Jaime I. There is still—in a chapel to the right of the nave—the statue of the Virgin which adorned the king's ship. Built in the 13th century on the site of a mosque, but transformed several times since, it retains of its original structure only the main façade and its noteworthy porch with very original statues, an essentially Majorcan Gothic piece of work.

Going round the church, we come to **Calle San Miguel,** a long medieval-looking street, very picturesque, with its flights of steps, its narrow squares and its baroque or Gothic churches. Calle Villanova opposite leads to the little medieval *Church of San Felipe de*

Neri and, farther on, to the *Church of La Merced* dating from the 18th century.

We leave again from Calle San Miguel, going south as far as **Plaza Mayor;** this is a typical 16th- to 17th-century Spanish square, showing the influence of Italian town planning which is found in all Spanish towns of the period; a rectangular *Plaza*, rather symmetrical, unlike the disorderly medieval square, lined with large arcaded houses, it is also a shut-off square which is reached through narrow alleys.

To get to know this part better, we have to go down the little flights of steps which lead, from the W of Plaza Mayor, to *Plaza Weyler*. At the far SW is the imposing façade of the *Berga Palace* with a grandiose *entrance* surmounted by the arms of the family and powerful caryatides. In the interior, a fine *patio* with a double staircase and first-floor loggia, the whole dating from the 18th century.

It is interesting to have a look at the north, from the other side of the square, through the little lanes (Calle Pueyo, Calle Campaner), then go back down through *Plaza Santa Catalina Tomàs* and the narrow streets—sometimes flights of steps—to the *Church of San Nicolás* (15th century). Beyond, past a very busy district of small shopkeepers and craftsmen, where we can see many picturesque interior courtyards and fine sculpted façades, we come to the little Renaissance *Church of Las Minonas* and the wide *Calle Jaime II*. We go down to the left to reach Calle del Conquistador and finally the Borne.

IV. The Lonja and the eastern districts

Going down the Borne towards the harbour, through *Avenida Antonio Maura*, we come to the **Paseo Sagrera** which runs along the sea; it is a lovely promenade with a wide terreplein planted with flowers and palm trees. The first building to which we come is the **Lonja** *(Exchange)*.

The erection of a building entirely for the merchants was envisaged immediately after Jaime I's conquest. But it was only in the 15th century that the need for it made itself felt and that the city could afford to put it up. *Guillermo Sagrera* was called in and most of the building is his work, though some of it was continued after he left for Naples and it was finally completed in 1451.

The Lonja is essentially a secular building, meant for business men, to be used both as a market for goods and bills and as a commercial tribunal. Entirely Gothic in conception, very simple and almost austere in its general impression, its decoration is already light and sophisticated, showing the influence of Italianism and the spirit of the Renaissance which were introduced by the Italian merchants who lived in the island.

The *façade* has a perfect elegance; it is adorned with soberly executed windows and a *roof gallery* with fine battlements using the curved line which is also found as a decorative motif in secular and military architecture in Italy at that time. The gallery is decorated also with *gargoyles*, surmounted from time to time by delicate little turrets and, at the corners, by four more imposing towers containing the spiral staircase by which the top is reached; one can go up one of the towers which offers a pleasant panoramic view of the harbour and old Palma.

The *interior* of the Lonja is much simpler. As in the nave of the cathedral, the architect impresses with his sobriety and boldness. The fine vaults above the nave and two aisles of equal height are upheld by two rows of spiral columns with prominent ribs, very delicately worked. They rise to a great height and no capital or entablature marks the juncture of the pillar with the crossing of the Gothic arches; just as the latter are set directly in the side walls without capitals or columns. The arches diverge in eight-part stars from the top of each column, thus forming six "palm trees". There are very unobtrusive medallions in the keystones of the arches.

This lay-out can also be found in the Lonja de la Seda of Valencia and in several monastery halls in the S. Mediterranean (Gothic era) and even in the naves of their churches which were as much meeting places as places of worship. This secular art seems to have been influenced by that of the religious orders, a characteristic of the reconquest in these southern countries.

The Lonja now houses the **Provincial Museum** which has a large collection of modern paintings and also numerous 15th- and 16th-century Gothic altar-pieces from churches in the island.

Beside the Lonja is the *Harbour Gate*, then the façade of the **Consulado de Mar.** This used to be a dependency of the Lonja, built in the 17th century to house the commercial tribunal. Its style is very different, much less pure and rather over-elaborate; but the *loggia* is very elegant with its richly decorated coffered wood ceiling, its stone balustrade and delicate columns with capitals which bear wide arcades; the rest of the façade is austere and without great interest.

Walking along the left side of this building we soon come to *Plaza de Atarazanas* with a fine fountain and a monument to *Jaime Ferrer*, the 15th-century Majorcan navigator and geographer. Turn into Calle San Pedro to the left of the square and then right into Calle San Lorenzo to get to the **Church of Santa Cruz.** The church of *San Lorenzo* used to stand on this site and now forms the crypt of the present building. It consists of a central square part with the high altar, surrounded by an ambulatory to facilitate the passage of the faithful and the access to the five chapels.

Santa Cruz is a church of the end of the Middle Ages, built over the crypt. The nave and two aisles and the apses date from the 15th century. The *façade*, dominated by a square belfry, bulky, with a pyramid-shaped roof, is the most recent part and has a rich porch worked in Plateresque style. From the exterior note also the squat apse, with three storeys, which looks like a fortress with its bulky buttresses stuck to the walls, its sparse, small windows and, crowning the wall, its battlements carved into steps. The interior has sumptuous gilt altars.

Take the continuation of Calle San Lorenzo, the *Calle de Santa Cruz*, then turn right into *Calle San Felio*, a very fine street which affords a grand view of old palaces as far as the Borne. On the left is an old chapel and along it runs *Calle Cayetano* with the *church* of the same name (18th century) and, above all, at No. 22 one of the façades of the **Palace of the Marquis of Sollerich** (also called **Morell Palace**); the other façade is on the Borne. This is doubtlessly the finest example of later Majorcan architecture.

It was built at the end of the 18th century. The most typical façade is the east one, facing the Borne. It comprises—Italian style—a wide arcaded *loggia* on the first floor; this is unusual for this kind of mansion which opened more often to the interior and showed only severe façades to the street and whose unobtrusive windows were its only apparent luxury.

The *patio* in the interior differs also from those of earlier periods; it is more open, more airy, with a high balcony, the bulky shafts of its columns and capitals with broad scrolls, its very cunning staircase, in two sections as far as the first landing, then joining into one: the wrought-iron railing is of a very delicate design.

EXCURSIONS ROUND PALMA

I. The western beaches and the suburbs

(30 km there and back by car; or by tram as far as Porto Pi.)

Leaving from the Lonja, take *Paseo Maritimo* which runs along the old ramparts beside the sea; beyond, we cross the suburb of **Santa Catalina,** an old fishing village that still has the ruins of the old windmills. Then comes the district of **Terreno,** very modern with its large hotels built since the beginning of this century, its fine promenades, shady parks and residential villas on the slopes of the hill. A little farther (4.5 km.), **Porto Pi** was a medieval harbour where the fleet of royal galleys anchored, shut in and sheltered by two strong towers, closed each evening by a heavy chain as was the custom in the olden days. Beside them, the modern fort of *San Carlos* (military zone).

The road moves a little away from the sea which, however, is still visible in glimpses between the villas and pines. The *Cala Mayor*, at Ca's Català (7 km) is a bathing centre (several little beaches) with good hotels in a picturesque setting. Farther on, houses become sparser, but the road runs often as a *corniche* (coast road) above the sea and affords an interesting drive. The coast, limestone rocks shaded by clumps of pines, is very jagged; numerous creeks with calm waters nestle at the foot of jagged headlands; they can easily be reached by small steep paths.

A slight detour along a little road on the right (9 km.) enables us to go to **Bendinat Castle.** It was here that King Jaime I the Conqueror is said to have sat down to a simple meal of garlic and olives with bread on the night after he had captured the city (in 1229) and, happy at his success on that glorious day, he is said to have cried: «I have eaten well» («bendinat»). The present castle was built in the 18th century in the midst of vast gardens; from the road we have many fine *views* of the coast and the city at the back of the bay.

The outskirts of Palma end, for the moment, at *Palma Nova* (14 km.), a large sandy beach with all manner of amenities.

II. Bellver Castle, Genova and Son Roca

Follow the same itinerary as far as Terreno where there is a road branching off to the right to the hill of **Bellver;** the castle may be reached by car along a winding road which runs between pinewoods; those on foot can take easy short-cuts.

The **castle,** a fortress to control the town and its lines of communication, was built by the second king of Majorca, Jaime II. He soon entrusted the work to his favourite architect *Pedro Salva* who also executed the Gothic buildings of the Almudaina. Situated at 490 feet above the sea, on an open site from which the whole bay and town are visible, the castle well deserves its name of Bellver (Fine View). It was often used as the royal residence, then became a prison for a long time before it was given to the city of Palma, in a perfect state of preservation.

It is a very fine example of military and princely architecture of Mediterranean gothic. The architecture doubtlessly was inspired by Catalan models, especially the Palace of Perpignan. But the castle's most surprising feature is its circular groundplan. It consists of severe sections and vaulted parts; huge halls on the

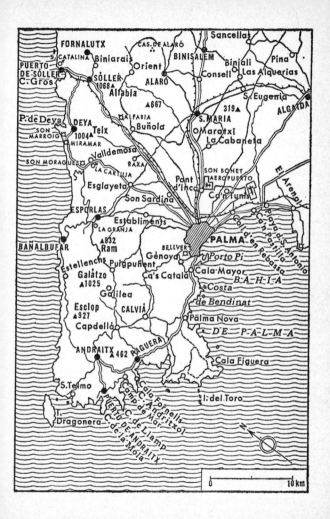

groundfloor, private rooms on the first floor, arranged in concentric circles round a central patio. This layout facilitates the draining of water—collected on roofs and terraces—into the central courtyard where there is an enormous cistern with its old wells. This "castle cistern" enabled the royal residence to solve the water problem which is so difficult in the whole of Majorca. Several bulky towers—rather curiously shaped—assured the defence of the fortress; the main one is the Tower of Homage, separated from the main structure like an isolated keep; a forward defence post, with its narrow windows and its forbidding crown of battlements, this tower reminds us of the military purpose of the buildings.

The *patio*, on the other hand, has a certain elegance and grace; above the semicircular arcades which are upheld by strong pillars on the ground-floor, the first floor forms a round frieze of much more delicate arches which cross and interlace at the top. The same impression of lightness, of trying to soften the severe effect, is found in the entrance where the apartments are adorned with slender stone pillars.

Behind the castle, on a higher hill, is the village of **Genova,** a classic excursion spot; you can get there either by tram or by a little road going up from the coast. Genova is a good centre for excursions into the mountains and you can also visit the strange *caves* hollowed out in the limestone. But the walk is particularly popular because of the ever wider *views* which the little road affords as it winds up the hill.

Another village on the foothills of the Sierra Burguesa, *Son Roca* (7 km. from Palma), also has some wonderful panoramic views of the city; you can go there by tram or by a road which leaves Palma on the N side (start from the Borne and Via Roma).

This road first goes through the hamlet of *Son Rapina*, a group of villas dominated by an old fortified watchtower, now attached to a lovely country house (*Son Cigala*). From this village a path on the left leads to another estate: *Son Vida*. These are the nearest of the great Majorcan country residences built in the 17th and 18th centuries for the rich families of Palma which are scattered along the heights and through the countryside; they are mostly still inhabited and cannot be visited.

III. The east coast

Leave Palma by the Lluchmayor road, then branch off to the right to the village of *Con d'en Rebassa* on the coast and the *El Arenal* beach (12 km. from Palma; also a fishing harbour). This excursion can also be made by train.

EXCURSIONS IN THE ISLAND OF MAJORCA

These excursions can all be made from Palma from where the main roads of the island diverge. The roads are often narrow but in a good state of repair. But skirting the coast along the coast road or the mountains is sometimes difficult, as along all the Mediterranean shores. The itineraries described below enable you to visit the most interesting parts of the island.

I. The Sierra Burguesa

Round trip of 56 km. on secondary, very hilly roads, but affording marvellous views all along the drive.

Leave Palma by Terreno and the Andraitx road. A little before Palma Nova (about 14 km. from the town) a little road branches off to the right which leads into the coastal mountain range which it crosses through pinewoods to reach *Calvià* (6 km. from the sea). A picturesque village and centre for walks through the mountains.

We can also get to Calvià by another road, though a slower one; this leaves from the Santa Catalina suburb of Palma and remains inland all the time; it goes over the *Sa Creu pass* at 1,480 feet altitude, through very lovely country with a superb *panoramic view* of Palma, the mountains and the bay.

Beyond Calvià, the road goes on to *Capdellà (Escapdello)* a little township dominated by the peaks of the Garaffa (to the SE) and of the Grua (to the N). From there a secondary road goes to Andraitx. It passes near *Son Cleret*, an imposing manorial estate in the midst of a rich domain.

Then comes a more hilly drive; we go up as far as *Galileà*, another village perched at a height of 2,000 ft. with a wonderful *view* across the pinewoods of the Sierra to the NE, culminating with Mount Galatzo at 3,360 feet. We go down to the valley of *Puigpuñent* (9 km. from Escapdello and 12 from Calvià), an agricultural township at the foot of the mountains, surrounded by orchards and olive groves.

From here a fairly easy, unsurfaced road leads north to the great estate of **Son Zafortezza**, a magnificent manorial residence whose gardens may be visited; groves, rivers and waterfalls, cleverly arranged fountains.

Beyond Puigpuñent the very picturesque road follows the valley of the Riera, then reaches Palma from the north, with fine *views* on Son Roca and the coast.

II. Andraitx and the south-west coast

(Round trip of 85 km.). Take the Terreno and Ca's Català road. At 15 km. from Palma, on the La Bataille pass, a *chapel* built to commemorate the first Mass said for the troops of Jaime I after they had landed nearby, in the little creek of *Santa Ponsa*.

Andraitx (30 km.) was—at an altitude of 436 feet— one of the fortified villages (a tower has survived inside the town) where the Majorcan peasants defended themselves against the Berber pirates, away from the coast which was too much exposed. Thus the harbour is 6 km. away, in a narrow bay overhung by imposing cliffs. Another little road leads to the *Oratory of Son Telmo* where stood the fortress which protected the town and from where we have a very fine *view* to the far end of Majorca and the adjacent island of Dragonera.

The tourist road which leads to the north coast from Andraitx was built at the beginning of this century; it climbs quickly to the rather arid plateau (altitude 1,310 feet) along which it continues through pinewoods. Then we skirt the sea along a very daring **coast road** (*corniche*) before reaching the amazing *view-point of Ricardo Roca*. **Estellènchs,** the only village on this wild but grandiose coast, is also slightly towards the interior, in a hollow planted with fruit trees (especially citrus).

The village is terraced up a steep slope, dominated by its square, flat-roofed *belfry*. In the surrounding country each field is irrigated; the water is carried by canals which follow a bold course down the steep mountain side, the canals being frequently covered by the stones set into the slopes. They are reminiscent of those of the "vega" of Granada. On the slopes and on non-irrigated terraces there are olive trees or the more dark-leafed carob-tree. The valley ends on the sea shore in a minute beach in a gap between cliffs, set among sheer rocks.

Beyond Estellènchs the road again follows the sea as a *corniche*. Sheer cliffs often assume strange shapes. Before coming to **Bañalbufar** (a village of small farmers and fishermen), we come to an old watchtower on a promontory: superb and extended *view*.

Here we come to a very different country: the barren, wooded slopes disappear and we seem to be in an oasis of freshness, with fields of early vegetables, orchards, clusters of pines outlining the cliff. It took a considerable effort to conquer and maintain this *huerta*; tiny, narrow terraces climbing up the steepest slopes, and everywhere reservoirs to hold the rain water or the water brought by the canals.

The road turns inland and we climb up a plateau. At 9 km. from Bañalbufar a little road to the left leads directly to Valldemosa (7 km. of rather difficult driving). A little farther on the right is **La Granja,** a vast farming estate founded by the Cistercian monks from Palma who had established an isolated farm there (a "grange"), where they raised sheep; it became subsequently the property of noble families who built (in the 17th century) a sumptuous residence in the midst of gardens with rockeries and ponds—a surprising luxury in a country where water is so scarce.

Beyond *Esporlas* we pass (at 16 km. from Bañalbufar) another great mansion at *Sarria* before arriving back at Palma.

III. Valldemosa, Soller and the north coast

Round trip of 85 km by road; Soller can also be reached by train, leaving from the Soller railway station N of Palma; the run, which takes about an hour, affords some very fine *panoramic views* over the valley and the distant sea, especially during the last part of the journey, going down to Soller.

Take first of all the Soller road and then, as soon as you are out of Palma, the road on the left to Valldemosa. The plain through which we travel is alive with the sound of windmills pumping water for the fields; then large almond orchards stretch farther than the eye can see. Finally, as we start up the first slopes of the northern Sierra, we come to lovely olive groves.

This excursion enables us to see the olive-growing region, so characteristic of the Majorcan countryside and for long the island's renown. The trees are many centuries old, with strange shapes, and stone-coloured contorted trunks. The whole life of the mountain people is devoted to the building and maintenance of a multitude of narrow terraces, supported by a stone wall; an exacting task requiring great skill.

After some uphill hairpin bends, the road goes down again to the valley of **Valldemosa,** green, with its fruit trees in the shade of clusters of palms. The village (19 km. from Palma) is a borough of 2,000 inhabitants, situated at an altitude of 1,380 feet, famed for its **Carthusian monastery.**

First of all King Sancho had a castle built, a sort of hunting rendez-vous; later Martin of Aragon gave the palace which he was no longer using to the Carthusians who made it into their monastery. It was founded in the 14th century by the monks from *Scala Dei* (in the S of Catalonia, near Tarragona). The monks lived in small cells near the Chapter House. The **chapel** is particularly noteworthy because of its interior decoration; carved wooden stalls and, in front of the inlaid altar, gothic *statues*, especially those of the altar *(Christ and Virgin)*.

In the 19th century, the Carthusian monastery was abandoned and the living quarters inhabited by private individuals, as they are still today. Thus *George Sand* stayed there in winter 1838 with her son, and *Chopin;* it was a very unhappy stay, yet "A Winter in Majorca" was written here and some of Chopin's Preludes. The three rooms have now been transformed into a *Museum* where some mementos have been preserved, but the most interesting item is the fine, rustic furniture.

Valldemosa is a pleasant holiday resort, a good excursion centre for the surrounding country and the mountains; the ascent of the *Puig du Teix* (3,550 feet)—quite difficult—must only be attempted in fine weather to get the extensive view over most of the island.

After Valldemosa the road climbs quickly to the ridge overlooking the sea (very fine **panorama** from the highest spot, 2 km.). Then we skirt along the coast by a narrow, winding *corniche*, one of the most fascinating drives in the island. There we come to the estate where Archduke Luis Salvador of Austria settled in 1860; he stayed there until his death, some fifty years later, captivated by the magnificent landscapes of this "costa brava", looking after the estate and its buildings. A scholar and writer, he was the greatest connaisseur of the island in his day and invited foreign scholars there.

The road passes close to the **Hospederia de Miramar,** built by the archduke to shelter travellers; from there an easy path leads through the wooded domain to the **Mirador de Miramar,** a sort of balcony attached to the cliff, which affords a marvellous *panorama*, especially to the N over La Punta de la Foradada, thrust far out into the sea.

One can also visit the archduke's two residences which are reached by two well-kept, tree-lined paths branching off the main road. That of **Miramar** was built on the site of a late 13th-century Franciscan College where Raymond Lull taught Oriental languages to those monks who were to go out and evangelize the Moslem countries. Of this period remains a *defence tower* and a part of the *cloister* brought from the Franciscan monastery at Palma (in the 14th century). The modern building is noteworthy for its furniture and its local collections (majolica). 500 yards farther on, on a steep rock, is a commemorative chapel called the *chapel of Raymond Lull*.

The path to the other residence, **Son Marroig** starts 2 km. farther along the road. This is one of the former properties of the great landowners of the island, built in the 16th century, serving both as a fortress and a mansion with its dependencies. A thick, massive *tower* survives from the old fortifications; subsequently modern buildings were added, especially a sort of little temple which affords a vast *panoramic view;* in the interior of the house, collections of local crafts (glass and porcelain) and items found during excavations.

The road leaves the sea and goes through the village of **Deyà** (40 km. from Palma); a township perched on a rock in an amazing position, with its old houses packed tightly along streets with steps, its sombre arches, and right at the top, its stronghold.

After Deyà we again approach the sea (very fine *view point* at the top) before going down by a long, steep road with many hairpin bends, amidst splendid olive groves, into the rich *valley of Soller*, a deep and fertile oasis between the highest mountains of the island. Following the windings of the road, we are faced in turn by the rocky coast and the sea, the imposing bulk of *Puig Mayor* (4,740 feet), the sierras to the south of the valley and, on the slopes, several villages with their tiny *huertas*. **Soller,** in the hollow of the valley, looks from a distance like a big wood of orange and lemon trees and next to each house are one or two palm trees.

Soller is the centre and agricultural market of this fertile valley (in Arabic the word *Sulliar* means "golden valley"). The town has only 12,000 inhabitants, yet it is the only one that in past centuries has known a really urban life and a bourgeois civilization similar to that of Palma.

The port was situated a few kilometres away because the peasants feared attacks from the sea and also because they preferred being nearer their fields. Here came the famous Soller *"balancelles"* (single-mast boats) to load the fruits and vegetables of the area. This export trade is now practically non-existent (the trees were not renewed and the sudden competition of Valencia practically ruined the market); it often led to emigration by the local population who accompanied their oranges abroad and became vegetable merchants in France (particularly in Marseilles). This tradition has survived. Even today the local inhabitants like to settle abroad and come back with a little fortune to build themselves a nice house.

A town of emigrants, Soller is a calm, somewhat sleepy place, clean and prosperous. There are a number of old houses, all alike, which have a great deal of character: tall grey façades, with wrought-iron balconies, narrow *patios* in the entrance, dark but welcoming, where rows of chairs are set out for visitors. The largest ones have special names: *Castellet, Ca'n Pons, Ca'n Prohom*. There is also the old 14th-century Franciscan monastery.

Soller is also a centre for **excursions** into the mountains. A pleasant trip can be made to *Fornalutx* by a well-marked path which is practicable only for walking (6 km. there and back); we go up the stream which flows between orange groves below the olive terraces, dominated by the bulk of the Puig Mayor. **Fornalutx** is a typical little isolated Majorcan mountain village, with strange peasant houses, its steep streets cut by flights of steps.

Another, more difficult excursion, takes us to the rocky gorges of the *Barranch* and *Gore Blau*, real steep canyons which are reached by the same path if we turn right after the hamlet of *Biniaraix* and follow another steep path cut into wide steps and paved with slabs of stone.

From Soller, too, we can undertake the ascent of the island's highest peak, the **Puig Mayor** (altitude 4,740 feet); 10 hours there and back, either by Fornalutx or by branching off at Biniaraix (enquire at Soller).

A 5 km.-long road (there is also a tram) leads to **Puerto de Soller** with its row of picturesque fishermen's houses at the back of little clear-cut, shut-off bay. The quays, which are now almost deserted, have some military buildings. It is a pleasant place to stay at, and a good centre for excursions into the interior. From the Mirador, on top of the cliff, there is a splendid *view* over the curve of the *puerto;* everywhere high paths afford marvellous panoramas over olive woods or the *maquis*-covered ridges.

A sea trip—a classic and indispensable excursion—enables us to see one of the boldest landscapes of the Majorcan "costa brava": the *Torrent de Pareys* (it takes more than an hour). All along the path of the boat we see a fine coastline with *calanques* (inlets): Cola, Tuent, La Calobra, separated by large promontories (Morro de na Mora, Morro de na Vaca). The narrowest is that in which the Torrent de Parreys culminates after flowing through an amazing limestone country, crossing almost the whole sierra and receiving another stream which comes down from the Puig Mayor. The *calanque* thrusts its way into the interior, increasingly narrow, between magnificent escarpments of a thousand or so feet in height and with fantastic shapes. Right at the back, on a shingle beach washed by beautifully clear water, grow thickets of stunted shrubs.

The road from Soller to Palma is very hilly; it rises by a long stretch of hairpin bends to the *Soller Pass* at 2,950 feet altitude. At 6 km. from the pass is the **Albufadia estate** (or *Alfavia*); Moorish in origin, it belonged to the Moor *Benah Abet* who rendered important services to Jaime I at the time of the reconquest; it then became the property of a Majorcan family who built a fine residence there at the end of the Middle Ages and laid out the gardens.

A beautiful avenue of plane trees leads from the road to the house, surrounded by orchards and terraces with orange trees and fountains. A pergola with stone pillars occupies the whole of the façade. Under the entrance arch we can still see a coffered Moorish ceiling richly decorated with inlays of rare woods. A cistern in the garden also dates from the Arab period.

The road reaches the central plain of the island near the castle of Aufaln, then of *Buñola*, going through olive groves. Then we come to the almond country. In passing, we should visit the gardens of the **Raxa estate** a little farther on; it was given by Jaime I the Conqueror to one of his first comrades-in-arms, the count of Ampuras. The late 18th-century castle is surrounded by terraces, gardens adorned with clumps of trees, statues and an ornamental lake. We arrive back in Palma, 32 km. from Soller.

IV. Pollensa, Formentor and the north-east of Majorca

Round trip of 170 km by road; there is also a railway to Inca, 30 km. from Palma; leave from the Majorcan railway station, near the Soller railway station.

Leave Palma by the main Inca road. The drive, though easy for the first 30 km., is not monotonous. We cross the central plain of the island with no hills except for an occasional mound with a castle or fortified monastery.

This plain is fully cultivated; market produce—vegetables, tomatoes, red peppers which in autumn hang in long garlands from the balconies of all the village houses. But water is scarce: the northern Sierra holds back the damp winds and the country had to be irtigated. Each farm—built of coarse stone—has its own cistern and canals fed by windmills. Their uneven, awkward wooden vanes stand out above massive stone towers, flapping like wings in the wind; a sort of simple fin which serves as a rudder keeps them in the line of the wind. Their blurred outline, the long dry stone walls, the spiky clumps of barbary figs broken by red and green fruit give the landscape its characteristic, somewhat strange appearance.

15 km. from Palma, **Santa Maria** is a big agricultural township to which the country produce is brought for sale (picturesque markets); the convent of *Santa Maria de La Real* has retained its 16th-century cloister, surrounded by wide, rustic arcades (a little road leads from there to Buñola and to the road from Palma to Soller). From Santa Maria we make the excursion to

Alaro and its castle (7 km. N); this was the site of one of the most famous fortresses built by the Majorcan kings, the *Castell del Rey;* its imposing ruins remain on one of the first peaks of the northern Sierra. A fine *view* over the plain (we can rejoin the main road at Consell, at 4 km. from Santa Maria).

Soon after this we come to a zone which, though still irrigated, is given over wholly to almond growing; in the spring the sight of thousands of trees in blossom, stretching to the horizon, set against the pure blue of the sky and the young shoots of wheat, is unforgettable. **Binisalem** produces some good wines. **Inca,** 30 km. from Palma, is the third town of Majorca, with 15,000 inhabitants. It is also a large agricultural centre, renowned for its fairs and markets; it used to produce famous ceramics, but this skill has been lost.

Here we branch off the main road to the left into the road leading to the monastery of Lluch (if you don't want to make this detour which is very interesting, not only because of the monastery itself but also because of the fascinating country through which you pass, continue along the main road and, 13 km. beyond Inca, take the road on the left to Pollensa; this direct itinerary is easier and quicker).

The little road from Inca to Lluch rises very steeply in sharp hairpin bends passing through olive groves and then pinewoods. We go through the villages of Selva, Caimari, then follow a narrow gorge before starting the climb to the *Gux Pass* (1,245 feet; very fine *view* to the east over the sierra and the far-off sea); then the road goes down to the **monastery of Lluch** (18 km from Inca).

Built in the 14th century on a spot where the Virgin appeared to a shepherd, it is now a pilgrimage place for the people of Majorca and the Spaniards who live in the island. The chief interest of the monastery lies in its position, the panoramic views of the surrounding country which it affords and the rural charm of its outbuildings. The large grassy square with an old fountain of three superimposed basins, the old stables on the right with their round-tile roof supported by big, rustic pillars, and the wide semicircular gates opening on to the country side provide a very picturesque *ensemble*. The present church—dating from the 17th century— is decorated inside with baroque paintings and stuccoes. In a little chapel whose door opens into the church is the wooden statue—darkened by age and very worn—of *Nostra Señora de Lluch*, much venerated by pilgrims.

Lluch is also a good centre for interesting excursions into the mountains.

Excursion to Escorca and La Calabra by car: 40 km. there and back, by a narrow, mediocre and rather difficult road. We must go back to the Inca road and take the road on the right to Escorca, through a wooded stretch which affords very fine *views*. *Escorca* is a simple mountain village from which we can see (near the fountain) the cleft of the Torrent de Pareys. Beyond the pass (at 2,360 feet) the road runs downhill through a magnificent landscape dominated by the nearby Puig Mayor. Then it climbs up another pass, still within sight of the Puig Mayor and of the Massanella (4,400 feet) before going down in long hairpin bends towards the coast which it reaches at the little fishing port of La Calabra near the opening of the *calanque* of the Torrent de Pareys.

From Lluch to Pollensa (20 km. of rather poor road) the drive takes us through strange country and affords extensive panoramas. At first we have the limestone mountains of the Sierra, cut by ravines and deep clefts, with their oddly shaped peaks in the region of the *Puig Tomir* (3,610 feet) round which the road runs closely. Then the long descent towards Pollensa offers at every turn wonderful and varied *views* over the bay and the Formentor peninsula which closes it to the

N. The last part of the drive goes through the green depths of the valley.

Pollensa (10,000 inhabitants) is a very old town in which the old Majorcan traditions have survived; women's costumes, regional dances, festivals on the occasion of pilgrimages, Christmas or the Carnival, and craftsmanship (especially rich embroideries on linen canvas). Like Soller, the town has its own characteristic look and a certain old-world charm, with its old houses of coarse stone built for the burghers, their narrow vaulted patios and massive façades. There are few noteworthy monuments, but note the present *Town Hall* installed in the former Jesuit monastery, the *Dominican monastery* and the 16th-century *San Jorge Oratory*.

The most interesting building is **Santa Maria del Puig,** situated on a height at about an hour's walk from the town. Of this former monastery—practically a fortress—there remains in particular the church with an *altar-piece* dedicated to the Virgin, a masterpiece of 15th-century Majorcan painting, still very Gothic in its inspiration and execution. From the church we have a fine *view* of the valley, the western mountains, the north coast and the bay of Pollensa.

EXCURSIONS

1. *To the Castillo del Rey* (footpath, about 3 hours' walk going in the earlier part by the ravine of Tornellas planted with holm-oaks). The strongest fortress in the island, magnificently situated on a lonely rock overlooking the sea from the height of a sheer cliff. After destroying the Arab castle, Jaime I built a new stronghold, a powerful military support to the dynasty of the Majorcan kings. It was here that Jaime III withstood successfully a long siege by the Aragonese in 1285 when they tried to capture the island. Only ruins survive: three gothic arches and the wall, partly with battlements. Unusual *view* to the west over the cliffs.

2. *To La Cala de San Vincente;* 12 km there and back by a little road. Very fine position; beach at the back of *a calanque* (inlet) bordered by steep rocks and pinewoods.

Leave Pollensa by the Formentor road. At 6 km.: **Puerto de Pollensa,** a little fishing port, facing south, at the foot of the Formentor peninsula in sight of the wide bay of Alcudia which is closed in by a large promontory. A pleasant resort: beaches, excursions to the peninsula, boat trips (services to the hotel of Formentor).

The road leaves the harbour and rises towards the crest; an easy yet impressive drive, skirting the coast all the time, with *wonderful views* of the bay of Pollensa, the north coast and particularly the *peninsula of Formentor* which continues far towards the NE. We go through a region of limestone scree, the only colour being in the thickets of prickly shrubs and tiny dwarf palm trees. Finally we go down to the little bay where the luxurious *Formentor Hotel* was built in 1930 (tennis, golf, beach, etc.).

The peninsula has preserved its lovely forests; there are a number of interesting walks along well-marked paths, both to the interior and the coasts. The *bay of La Posada* is very sheltered, bordered by thickets, and has a beautiful long beach of fine sand; it is equipped with exotic straw sunshades. From the hotel there are motorboat trips, especially to the *Cabo de Formentor* whose high, coloured cliffs are dominated by the lighthouse, the goal of the excursion (distance from Puerto de Pollensa: 21 km.).

We return to Puerto de Pollensa (the trip can be made by boat one way, by foot the other). Then we follow the little recently built road which runs along the bay and leads to **Alcudia.**

This tiny town (4,000 inhabitants) is one of the oldest in the Balearic Islands. At first a Phoenician colony, a port of call used by the Orientals during their voyages through the Tyrrhenian sea, it was subsequently conquered by the Romans. It was at that time called *Pollentia* and dominated the whole northern part of Majorca, thanks to its advantageous position between its two ports which—guarded by fortified strongholds on either side of the isthmus—enabled the Romans to send supplies to the town at all times.

Only some vestiges of the town walls survive from that great era, as well as an *antique theatre* which shows——as in Provence—clear traces of oriental influence. From the time of the Arab domination, on the other hand, nothing has survived although the town was the capital of the island. The Christian reconquest turned it into a stronghold and soon surrounded it with new walls; from this time date the two large gates in the present ramparts: the *El Muelle Gate* with its two massive towers and the smaller *San Vincente Gate*. Churches, too, were built: that of Santa Ana is one of the earliest of reconquest times; it is in a very simple style of primitive Majorcan Gothic, with a plain nave. There are also some old medieval houses in Alcudia.

Excursions in the surroundings: 1. *to the puerto*, a little road to the south. 2. to the north, the little *port* of the *bay of Pollensa* with a pleasant view of the Formentor peninsula. 3. on foot (1½ h there and back): *Mal Pas* viewpoint from which the coast can be seen. 4. to the *Albufera*, in the south (a little road, about 8 kms there and back). The Albufera is a long inland lagoon separated from the sea by a coastal strip. It is a marshy, unhealthy region once used only by reed-gatherers and hunters of wild fowl; the development of rice-growing (as in the Albufera of Valencia) has transformed this region and brought it a certain measure of prosperity.

From Alcudia we take the direct road to Palma which penetrates the interior and crosses the whole length of the central plain. Here too we find a skyline crowded with countless simple windmills used to pump the water for the market produce, especially tomatoes.

On the slopes and in the less irrigated parts there are vineyards and fig-trees. At 11 km. from Alcudia a little road on the left leads to **La Puebla.**

This peasant borough was founded in its entirety by Jaime I after the Reconquest in order to house a group of Catalans in search of arable land; the little town has the regular lay-out and the well-planned street typical of colonised villages in the southern countries.

2 km. farther another road, to the right, goes to the borough of **Campanet,** well-known for its church, the perfect example of the medieval Majorcan country church.

San Michele of Campanet is a very simple building, believed to date from the 14th century, and has a very rustic appearance: a single nave with no side windows, surmounted by a short arcaded belfry which is not lacking in elegance, covered by a roof with round tiles.

Then the road goes on to Inca (26 km. from Alcudia). From Palma to Inca, see above, p. 62.

V. Manacor and the caves of the east coast

Round trip by road 190 km. there and back; from Palma, trains to Manacor and Arta.

Leave the town by the eastern road which is the one going to the airport. Soon after the suburbs it goes through the rich *huerta* of the central plain with its typical vegetable fields and windmills. At 15 km. from Palma we quickly cross a first line of hills; beyond them the country is a little different; the plain is no longer uniform but dominated here and there by more prominent heights, usually from 490 to 985 feet high: poor peaks, with no character and no vegetation. Apricot and peach orchards increasingly take the place of market produce.

Algaida, 23 km. from Palma, is situated on a height, and on market days all the produce of the country is brought there. In the little town a road to the right leads south to the **Monastery of Randa** (6 km.).

The hill of **Randa** dominates the whole region; from the peak (altitude 1804 feet) there is an extensive *view* over the central plain and the Sierra which closes the horizon to the N; to the W and S we see the sea (on clear days the bay of Palma is visible). Since the time of the reconquest this has been a centre of pilgrimage and the Franciscans have established themselves here; Raymond Lull who lived there for ten years, teaching Arabic, set up a College similar to the one on the Miramar estate (near Deyà—see above p. 58) to train missionaries to Islam. Now only the *Monastery of Cura* survives on the summit and, lower down, that of *NS de Gracia* which was built at the end of the Middle Ages.

Beyond Algaida the main road passes close to *Montuiri*, a large perched village with an old medieval convent and some vestiges of ramparts which can be seen on the left. Then we come to *Villafranca* and, at 52 km. from Palma, to **Manacor,** the second city of the island, with 25,000 inhabitants, and the great market for the eastern regions. There are fairs and markets, wine cellars and warehouses, and recently established factories of artificial pearls of which varied samples are exhibited in the shops on the church square.

The town was already a rural centre at the end of the Roman Imperial period, at the time when Christianity established itself in the island; in the immediate surroundings we can still see the remains of the Christian *Son Pereto* basilica, already a fairly large building which testifies to the prosperity of the region. There were some interesting *mosaic pavings* and some *sarcophagi* which have been preserved in the Manacor Museum, in the Torre du Puntas (see below). Later Manacor became one of the residences of the Majorcan kings who built one of their fortified palaces there, dominating the flat countryside and protecting the island from pirate raids; only a *tower* and some vestiges of walls survive of the castle.

The baronial families also fortified their country mansions in the surroundings; the lords would shelter all their household there and at times of an alert would retreat there with their tenants. Near the town we can still see two defence towers with fine battlements; the **towers** of *els Anagistes* and *de Puntas;* the latter is less austere and shows some attempt at comfort and a certain elegance which marks the transition from military gothic art to a more sophisticated civilian art at the beginning of the Renaissance; there are twin windows with fine marble columns. The **monastery of Manacor** was built by the Dominicans; late cloister (18th century) in two storeys with rich baroque decoration.

The Manacor region is known to the tourist especially for its **limestone caves** which form the object of many organized excursions. The water easily infiltrated into the limestone soil and formed subterranean rivers which, as they approached the sea, carved out great hollows, often separated by waterfalls, where they became real lakes. The most fascinating are undoubtedly the caves of Drach, but all those open to the public are worth visiting.

1. The Caves of els Ham. Take the road which runs east to Porto Cristo and, after about 10 km., a little road to the right leading to the caves of els Ham (visit with a guide, admission fee). They are formed by an old underground river of which only small, residual lakes remain.

The caves are arranged in a series of "rooms" where the waters have left whitish chalky deposits, sometimes with ochre or yellow tints, which assume strange shapes; in each room stalactites and stalagmites create a fairyland of pillars, pinnacles, fantastic masses, outlines of animals and plants. These mineral formations are tremendously varied, and it is difficult to name each "room" so as to convey the vagaries of its decor; there is a *Lagoon Room*, a *Palace Room*, a *Witches' Room* and, above all the Room of the *Angel's Dream*, the largest and most impressive.

2. The Caves of Drach and Porto Cristo. Quite near Porto Cristo (12 km. from Manacor) a road quickly leads to the caves of Drach. They have been known and visited since the end of the 19th century and they were explored by the great French geologist and speleologist E.A. Martel who also explored the Gouffre (pothole) of Padirac and the Canyon of Verdon. These caves extent over 2 km.; they have been equipped for visitors and fitted with electric light which enhance the unearthly appearance of some of the "rooms" and the reflection of the stalactites in the lake waters. The visit takes more than an hour (nearly 2 hours on Sundays).

The general appearance is much the same as that of the caves of Ham, but the rooms are usually much bigger and the colonnades and pillars more imposing. There are several caves which consist of two or three rooms each. Thus, we see in turn: the *White Cave* with its two tiny lakes (Lake of Wonders and Lake of Delight) and the *Virgin of the Pillar*, a monumental stalagmite of astonishing shape; the *Black Cave* which owes its name to the traces left on walls and ceiling by the smoke of torches, the *Luis Salvador Cave* which is the most famous of all. We cross a number of narrow passages to get to the *Martel Lake*, discovered by the scholar in 1896 and almost 200 yards wide. The visit to the caves includes a boat trip on this lake enabling the visitor to see certain lighting effects and reflections in the water (in parts it reaches a depth of 33 feet); on some days the visitors sit on benches and listen to a concert given by musicians passing by in boats. The last cave is called the *Cave of the French* with some fine examples of clusters of columns.

Porto Cristo is a little fishing port, perfectly sheltered in a deep creek, at the foot of high chalk cliffs; there are several pleasant hotels and restaurants.

3. Arta and its surroundings.

At 20 km. from Manacor, **Arta** is a picturesque little town which has preserved its typical medieval appearance. The town, situated on the slope of the hill, has narrow, winding paved streets, lined with old patrician houses; it is dominated by the old castle stronghold built on the height from which there is a fine *view* of the surrounding country and the NE coast.

The surroundings of Arta were inhabited long before the occupation of Majorca by the Phoenicians. Here we find the best preserved *talayots*, huge structures which are doubtlessly proof of an indigenous civilisation.

The most famous of these monuments is in the immediate surroundings of the town; this is the talayot of *La Canoca*, a sort of defensive building of heavy stones in a picturesque setting. Another talayot is 8 km. from Arta to the W, near the little road which runs round the bay of Alcudia by the interior. From Arta, too, an unsurfaced road leads N to the little *chapel of Benem*, set in country of heath and shrub, standing on a rock which overlooks the sea, facing the whole bay and promontory of Alcudia.

The north-east coast, which has great sheer cliffs, is not easily accessible, but beyond Arta the main road bends towards the west and leads (after 10 km) to **Capdepera,** another old little town which has retained a good deal of character.

On the top of the hill there is a fine *fortified wall* dating from the time of the reconquest, with massive defence towers. The upper town is in ruins; there remains only a *chapel* and some vestiges. But lower down, on the slopes, there are more modern houses in a pleasant setting.

The road goes on to the sea which it reaches at the *Cala Ratjada* (2 km.), a small creek, well sheltered by the cliff which is surmounted by a lighthouse; there are pleasant walks leading up to the lighthouse.

From Capdepera another, less good, road branches off to the SW to rejoin the one (3 km.) which leads to the **Caves of Arta** (10 km. from Arta). These caves open —towards the sea— in the side of a sheer cliff (very fine view from the entrance of the coast towards the S).

These caves have been known for a very long time (since the 17th century); now they are perfectly equipped for visitors with lighting effects —sometimes coloured— and show a great variety of artificial landscapes. There are not, as at Hams or Drach, underground lakes or rivers (the river has completely disappeared from the caves which it hollowed out) but there are wonderful forests of stalactites and stalagmites of extraordinary shapes. The dimensions of the rooms are often imposing, particularly in the famous *Room of the Standards* (165 feet high) where immense draperies of limestone from the vault give the impression of an array of flags.

Returning into the interior, we soon take a little road to the *Torre de Canamel* the former look-out and defence post against the Saracens.

Back at Arta, we can return directly to Palma by the road along which we came. If we want to avoid going back the same way, we can stop overnight on the way (for instance at Porto Cristo) and take the Felanitx road from Manacor which enables us to combine this round trip with the excursions to Lluchmayor and Santañy (see below).

VI. Lluchmayor, Santañy and the south-east

(120 km. there and back; train from Palma to Felanitx and from Palma to Santañy by Lluchmayor.)

Leave Palma, from the SE, by the Lluchmayor road which turns away from the sea and crosses the Majorcan countryside in a straight line. It rises steadily to a sort of chalky plateau with some rounded peaks. **Lluchmayor** is a large rural borough, 23 km. from Palma, at the centre of an irrigated region, with apricot and peach orchards (food preserves, jams). It was also one of the first inhabited centres in the island and there are still some imposing pre-Roman buildings, remains of gigantic walls which surrounded real entrenched camps. At 1 km. from the town are the wall and towers of *Son Julia*, and the more imposing ones of *Capucorp Vell* situated 13 km away.

Past Lluchmayor the road becomes more winding and slower; it goes first through *Campos* (15th-century chapel and, nearby, the hermitage of San Blas). Then we come to **Santañy** (26 km.), a little agricultural town, isolated at the far end of the island in a pleasant, wooded country; some parts of the medieval *ramparts* survive from the time when the town—built in haste to house the Catalan colonists —had to defend itself against pirates. As in all Majorcan coastal areas, the fortified village was built a few kilometres from the sea which is now reached by a little road leading to a well-sheltered creek at the foot of a pine-covered cliff with an old watch tower, the *Torre d'en Beu*.

From Santañy a little road climbs up the plateau to the N, then—by a hilly and varied itinerary—leads to **Felanitx** (16 km.), another small rural capital. It, too, is a large peasant village founded at the time of the reconquest to colonize, at 10 km from the nearest creek, this sparsely populated part of the country. Today Felanitx is chiefly famous for its vineyards which yield renowned wines, its large almond orchards, and its pottery works which have an old popular tradition. In the vicinity there are troglodyte monuments and dwellings *(Cavas des Bous)*.

The most interesting excursion, however, is the one to the **Monastery of San Salvador** (5 km.) by a little road which climbs up the hill (1,640 feet) after passing in front of the ruins of

Santueri Castle, an impressive Arab stronghold. The Monastery, founded at the end of the Middle Ages, was rebuilt in the 17th century. From the terrace, a wonderful *panoramic view* of this whole part of the island, with its mountains, and to the east over the chalky coast.

From Felanitx an unsurfaced road leads to *Puerto Colon* (15 km.), a small fishing and coastal traffic port.

We can return to Palma by various routes: the most direct is through Campos and Lluchmayor, others lead to the main road from Manacor to Palma. We can also first go from Felanitx to **Porreras** by another little road, in a rather poor state of repair, but passable (13 km.).

Porreras is a colonized town built at the end of the 13th century for Catalonian immigrants. It was one of the best wheat areas in Majorca, source of the island's famous flour; there are still numerous windmills. On a hill, a little outside the village, a Gothic *chapel* in a picturesque position from which we overlook the plain.

To the N of Porreras the road rejoins the main route after 6 km and comes out opposite Montuiri.

MINORCA

THE COUNTRYSIDE

Minorca is the most northerly of the Pityusae; it is situated at 35 km. NE of Majorca, more exposed to the sea winds. It is smaller, being only about 50 km. (31 miles) from east to west, with an area of hardly 700 square km. Minorca is very different from the other islands of the Archipelago. It is not mountainous, but a "flat island" level with the horizon. It is true that there are some hills in the N, with deep valleys; but even the highest peak, Mount Toro is only 1,165 feet high. The whole southern part is a vast limestone plateau, a sort of flat land with sparse grass. The produce has neither the richness nor the variety of that of the Majorcan mountains and plains. Here the sea winds reign supreme since no mountain barrier protects the interior.

The winds are so regular and so strong that they have given their names to the two main regions of the island. In the N is the **country of the Tramontane,** a violent wind which comes directly from the Gulf of Lions; the irregularity of the relief creates a certain diversity: poor produce, pasture land, often pinewoods on the heights. In the S is the **Mitjorn**, named after the south wind, less damp but also less violent. The country is cut up into a multitude of little enclosures shut in on all sides by walls of dry stones. Seen from above the plain looks like an endless mosaic of irregular squares, cut through by winding paths, with here and there the dazzling white of a village. There are no trees (except near the sea, on the cliffs of the inlets); the shrubs only grow to the height of the walls (3 to 6 feet), then bend to the direction of the prevailing wind. In the shelter of the walls grow some vegetables or thin rows of fodder.

Minorca has no pronounced maritime character. It rises sheer from the sea, without transition, in steep cliffs. A picturesque coast, especially in the N, indented by real fjords with wooded shores which run deep into the interior. The S coast is straighter and affords less natural shelter. However, the banks have their backs to the land, for it is not easy to climb up the plateau: two active ports are the only big towns in the island: Mahon and Ciudadela.

Stock-farming is almost the sole resource of the inhabitants. In the drier hilly parts there is sheep breeding; in the Middle Ages Minorcan wool was highly valued throughout Mediterranean markets. Since then cattle breeding has developed considerably in both parts of the island. In the S the animals move from one enclosure to the next in search of fresh pasture and water which is collected in huge cisterns.

The Minorcan country house is a farmstead with immense outbuildings for storing fodder and housing the animals. Sometimes the stables are in the midst of the fields, making temporary shelters, but they are always in the vicinity of a rain-water cistern. They often have curious shapes: modest white-washed cubes without windows or even simply heaps of dry stones, set out in concentric circles in the shape of tiered cones, resembling the earliest structures in the island. Minorca is also famous for its cheeses, particularly the well-known "mahonesa"; stock-raising has created an important leather industry, the only appreciable craft or industrial activity in the island; a large proportion of Spanish shoe manufacture is concentrated in Majorca and Minorca.

But this rather archaic economy has never brought the Minorcan people an adequate livelihood. Hence the emigration of the island's peasants in search of richer lands; they have colonized whole cantons in Algeria in the region of Oran (especially near S. Bel-Abbès); there were also many near Algiers in the large market-garden suburbs.

MAHON

The capital of Minorca is a little town of 25,000 inhabitants, built on a remarkable site. It is famous for its roadstead which is splendidly protected; it is a long sound almost 5 km long, very narrow and easy to defend, dominated by high cliffs and protected by the forward islands (Isla de la Cuarentena, Isla de la Ratas, Isla de Pinto, Isla del Rey which the troops of Alfonso III took by assault in 1282). The main inlet at whose back the town lies, has a ramification of sub-

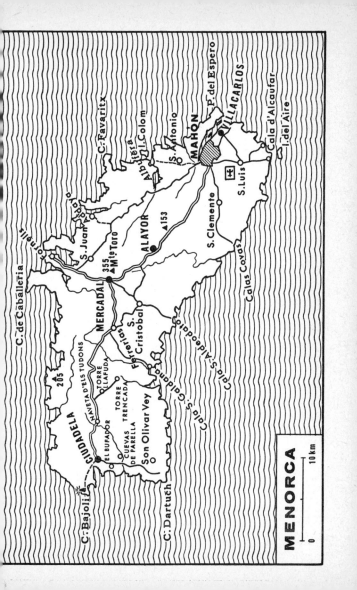

sidiary arms and the whole is reminiscent of the *rias* of Brittany (e.g. the roadstead of Brest).

Its position has always given Mahon the reputation of an unassailable military port. The Carthaginians and, much later, the Arabs had established a stronghold there to secure their lines of communication in the Mediterranean and to be used as a springboard for their raids on enemy convoys. Mahon did not share in the growth of traffic during the Middle Ages which Palma enjoyed; it remained provincial, its life more shut in, called upon occasionally to receive the king's squadrons or to export the island's local produce. It did not experience a golden age of Catalonian or Majorcan trade. Moreover, Minorca bore, in the 16th century, a continous series of attacks by Berber pirates who came from the African coast; neither the harbour's fortifications nor the look-out posts (the old *abalayas* of the coast) could prevent the raids, and twice the Algerian Turks made war on it; in 1535 Barberousse sacked Mahon and later the fleet of Selim II under the command of Mustapha Piali ran aground outside Mahon which was then defended by a new fort (San Felipe, built in 1534), but Ciudadela was taken and sacked.

It was in the 18th century that its military character assumed the greatest importance when the Spaniards, helped by the French, disputed the port with the English. Mahon suffered a number of long sieges; during the most famous, that of 1756, the roadstead was blocked by a squadron of twenty French ships under the command of the Duke of Richelieu; the French were able to disembark and assault the town.

Mahon, a completely white town, dominated by the spires of its belfries, rises from the sea on a white chalky table-land above the waters of the harbour, which—coming from the quays—is reached by a sort of ravine. This natural defence was formerly reinforced by a strong ring of ramparts.

Tour of the town

The centre of the old city is **Plaza España.** From the harbour it is reached by a flight of steps; by car, one has to make a detour along the alleys which climb up the slope of the ravine. From Plaza España turn W to *Plaza de la Conquista* where there is a statue of King Alfonso III.

At the side of the square is the *Palace of Museums, Archives and Libraries;* a façade with pediments and columns; inside, collections of paintings and coins. Nearby we can see the **Church of Santa Maria** which was built during the period immediately following the reconquest (13th century), but was completely rebuilt in the 18th century. In the nave: monumental organ, tombs of two French governors of the island and sumptuous high altar with heavy canopy.

Opposite the church, on Plaza del Generalísimo Franco, is the **Town Hall** *(Ayuntamiento)* where the notables of Minorca met to decide local questions; it was also called the "Sala" or the "Casa Consistorial". The building was begun at the start of the 17th century (in 1613) but was also transformed in the 18th century. The arcaded façade has fine balconies with wrought-iron railings; in the interior, a collection of paintings (portraits). The Gothic *Church of San Francisco,* just beside it, is built on a terrace overlooking the harbour. From Plaza del Generalísimo we can go up as far as the *San Roque Gate,* a former fortification of the ramparts.

Leaving again from the centre, Plaza d'España, but this time to the E, we go to *Plaza del Carmen* with the *Carmen Monastery;* we can still see the *church* built in the 18th century; an immense interior with several valuable works of art, including the famous Gothic *Virgin of Seafarers.* Now the market is held in the monastery's former cloister. To the south of the church a fine *promenade* runs along the sea overlooking the harbour. Then we follow Calle del Carmen to the E to get to *Plaza José Antonio* with the Museum of Natural Science housed in the *Ateneo Palace* (collection of animals) which also has a large section on local traditions (and Minorcan costumes).

EXCURSIONS IN THE SURROUNDINGS
OF MAHON

1. The roadstead. This is seen by the visitor on arrival, but a special boat trip enables us to see the most interesting parts again and to visit the small shady creeks with their pinewoods (especially *Cala Figuera*, a popular trip). We can also, by road or path, visit some of the villages along its picturesque coast. Recommended itineraries:

a. *San Antonio;* leave Mahon by the N and go round the roadstead across the wooded hills. 3 km., San Antonio; fine view of the harbour of Mahon and its line of white houses at the back of the bay; at the Golden Farm, mementos of Nelson's stay. 2 km. beyond San Antonio, the pleasant beach of *Cala Mezquida*.

b. *Villa Carlos*; 4 km from Mahon, on the opposite shore. It used to be the residence of English officers in the 18th century (it was then called George Town), in a pleasant position.

2. San Luis and the south coast. Take the little road which leaves Mahon to the S. We cross the Mahon country, cut through by winding paths between dry stone walls. 4 km. *San Luis*, a strange peasant village which was founded in the 18th century opposite Villa Carlos by the French after the capture of Mahon by the Duke of Richelieu, to house the Breton sailors; we can still see the *fleur de lys* on the façade of the church. The township has retained a very picturesque appearance, in the midst of minute fields and windmills, with its low, white-washed houses (San Luis is the "ciudad blanca") which present only severe, massive façades broken by a single door, to the street.

Beyond San Luis, the little road goes on as far as the *calanque of Alcaufar* which is very popular with the citizens of Mahon who build country villas there.

3. The Albufera and the north coast. (10 km. from Mahon); comparatively difficult access by a small unsurfaced road. The *Albufera*—like the Alcudia at Majorca—is a salt-water pool, a fishing and hunting area; beyong the coastal strip is a fine sandy beach shut in by a little island.

4. San Clemente. The road goes E from Mahon and first passes near the *talayot of Torello*, one of the most impressive megalithic monuments in the island. It is an enormous tower, roughly conical in shape; it was doubtlessly a funeral monument which was used as a defence post in the Middle Age and as late as the 17th and 18th centuries.

San Clemente (5 km. from Mahon) is a typical little peasant village. The road goes on for another 3 km.; we overlook the south coast above steep inlets *(Calas Covàs)* which we reach by sheer paths. There are numerous *caves* hollowed out of the side of the cliff which overlooks the sea. These "cavas", originally cave dwellings, are often found in the cliffs along this coast, but those at San Clemente are the most easily accessible.

CIUDADELA

At the other end of Minorca, Ciudadela was for a long time the true capital of the island, from the time of Moorish domination and later under the Majorcan and Aragonese kings. Some economic activity and a prosperous bourgeoisie grew up there. From this period the town has kept not only its cathedral and impressive episcopal palace, but also a number of baronial residences whose fine façades and stately, severe appearance remind us of the palaces of Soller or Palma. These were the homes of the large Minorcan landowners whose fortunes were derived from sheep raising and the export of wool to Italy. But these people lived far from the Majorcan court and their tastes remained simple and austere.

The English, anxious to remain near the port of Mahon where they were entrenched, deprived Ciudadela of its rôle as capital. At present, however, it is the centre of the island. With 12,000 inhabitants, it is a pleasant little town, picturesque in parts, with interesting mementos of the past. On the shore of a small, well-protected bay, lie the town's quays where are moored large boats that engage in coastal traffic to Mahon and especially to the north of Majorca. Of its old, strongly fortified ramparts only some vestiges remain; but the old town which they enclosed has kept its medieval appearance with its streets with porches and its neatly-arranged old façades. Ciudadela is particularly animated on the feast day of St John which is celebrated annually with medieval traditional processions and folk dances, games and performances of traditional scenes.

The town

Its centre is the **cathedral,** on the site of the old Arab mosque which was converted for Christian worship at the time of the reconquest. As at Palma, the building of the new church was undertaken much later (begun only a century later and continued until the beginning of the 15th century). The façade was subsequently rebuilt, as were also the side chapels, partly in the 16th century, partly as late as the 19th (from this period date the neo-classic parts of the building).

The *interior*, very sober, with a single nave and modest but pleasant in size.

The other centre of urban life was the *Governor's Palace*, the *Alcazar* of Moorish days, a powerful fortified dwelling which overlooked the town and the harbour. Now it is the **Ayuntamiento** whose façade occupies one side of the lovely *El Borne* Square. The latter has a fine group of patrician dwellings: some houses (particularly the *Torresaura Palace*) have interior patios with the windows and loggia giving on to them.

We return to the cathedral from which—to the E in the continuation of the apse—branches the *main street of the old town*, very characteristic with its booths under arcades and its large paving stones. Nearby are the most interesting churches of Ciudadela: the 17th-century *Convento de San Agostino*, the *Church of San Cristo* and the *Rosario Church*, with a fine, richly decorated baroque porch.

Surroundings of Ciudadela

1. *Naveta d'els Tudons;* 2 km. from the main Mahon road. The *naveta* is a funeral monument in the shape of an upside-down vessel, dating from the earliest Balearic civilisation; it is particularly well preserved and easily accessible.

2. *Bajoli Lighthouse;* reached by an unsurfaced road; the lighthouse overlooks the N-E end of Minorca; fine *panorama*.

The road from Mahon to Ciudadela

44 km by the island's only major road; but there are some interesting detours, especially in the region of Mercadal. The road leaves Mahon in the NE and at once climbs up the plateau. At 5 km we pass near the taula of *Talati de Dalt*, a megalithic monument in the shape of a table *(taula)* which is made of a large stone resting on two upright stones.

The taula was at the centre of a sacred enclosure covered with stones where religious ceremonies and sacrificies took place. It is the most interesting monument of its kind in the Balearic islands. There is another a little farther, 10 km. from Mahon, the *taula de Torrauba*.

Alayor (12 km.) is a rural town which has remained quite picturesque *(Church of San Diego* with cloister). The road then passes near another megalithic monument, the *tower of Gaumès*, a bulky, impressive building. **Mercadal** (21 km) is the town of the interior, dominated by Minorca's highest peak, the *Mont Toro* (1,165 feet).

Excursions in the surroundings: footpath to the top of Mont Toro whence there is a fine *panorama* over the whole island and the very indented N coast. A little road leads to *Fornels* (8 km. N), a picturesque fishing port and a pleasant place for a stay, at the entrance of a deep bay; very pretty position, with a very extended view over the coast and, to the W., over the impressive headland of the *Cabo de Caballeria;* walk to the ruins of *Sanicera*, a Phoenician town.

A small secondary road leads directly from Mahon to Fornels without going through Mercadal (23 km.). It enables us to go along the Albufera and to approach the creeks which are very picturesque and which can be reached by footpaths; e. g., the bay of *Castells* with a fine beach shaded by pine trees, and that of

Addaya where there is a tiny fishing port with white-washed houses; rejoin the Mercadal-Fornels road.

From Mercadal we can also get to the coast much farther W with the inlet of *Pregonda* (10 km.) where there are also woods and a beach.

Beyond Mercandal the Ciudadela road leads to Ferrerias, an agricultural town founded by the king of Majorca after the reconquest. A little farther a road to the left takes us on the renowned excursion to the Barranco (ravine) of *Algendar:* about 4 km. by car, then on foot by the back of the *Barranco* as far as the creek of Santa Galdana, to the N of the sea (7 hours' walk). 15 km. from Mercadal another road to the left leads to the group of prehistoric monuments of *Torre Llafuda*. We finally come back to Ciudadela after passing near the naveta of *els Tudons* (see above).

IBIZA

ITS ORIGINALITY

Ibiza which belongs to the southern group of the Pityusae is about mid-way between Majorca and the continent, at 70 km. S-W of Majorca (7 h by boat from Palma and 8 h from Valencia). It is much smaller than the other islands: it has an area of only 575 square km. and is barely 30 km. north to south, at its greatest length. Its relief is rather like that of Majorca and there is a chain of mountains, the continuation of the Majorcan Sierra, which is found again farther south in the highlands of the Cap de la Nao (40,000 inhabitants)

Ibiza is thus a very mountainous island. True, the altitudes remain relatively small, the highest peaks rarely being more than 1,300 feet (1,558 at the Atalayasa, to the west of the capital). But its features are very pronounced; they are those of a Mediterranean sierra, with its chalky heights covered with pinewoods and a thick heath of juniper trees; many valleys cut through the island and as many tiny cantons, often isolated, opening to the sea only by a deep creek between high cliffs. The country is extremely varied and changes more suddenly even than in Majorca; here we don't find any large olive plantations nor plains with almond trees as far as the eye can see; there is a whole mosaic of different produce: orange orchards at the back of irrigated valleys, higher up fig trees, then, with woodland, pastures and fields of cereals. There is no large town apart from the capital; the peasants are dispersed, each family being isolated on its farmstead near its fields. Like the north of Majorca, Ibiza faces the sea from a sheer coastline, very indented and contorted. The W coast in particular consists of high cliffs which drop sheer to the sea, thrusting up numerous tiny islands, which were advanced defence posts and on which there are now lighthouses.

Ibiza occupies a place apart in the Balearic group of islands; it owes its originality to its past and to the part which the sea has always played in its life. For a long time it was an important Phoenician—then Carthaginian—trading centre, and assumed the features of Oriental civilizations. Archaeological excavations have brought to light numerous proofs of Punic occupation, e.g.

at the necropolis of the Puig dels Molins, at that of Es Cuyeran where little statuettes and Oriental divinities were found, and also at Plana. Throughout the centuries the Oriental influence has remained very much alive and is still recognizable today in many features of local life. First of all, in the costumes which recall those of Greece and of the Middle East; for men, wide white trousers, drawn in tightly at the ankle, shirts with puffed-out sleeves and the long knitted red cap; for women, embroidered shawls, scarves and handkerchiefs *(panuelos de cabeza* or *panuelos de mano)*, and jewels; fine filigree gold items and heavy ceremonial gold necklaces. Music and dances are also very individualistic. The houses, too, differ from those in the other Balearic islands. They are simple, white-washed cubes, sometimes even whitened with blue, one-storeyed with narrow windows, and flat terra-cotta roofs; these houses are found everywhere in the island and also along the coast in the form of simple, primitive huts where the fishing tools are kept.

Ibiza is the only one of the Balearic Islands which has always had a definite maritime character; to the sea it owes its resources and essential activities. Each peasant is also a sailor; he often goes down to the creek of his village where he keeps his boat which he can build or repair himself with the timber from the pinewoods that overlook his fields. True, the island has never known any great commercial peak period, and its inhabitants have not travelled up and down the world's great sea routes; the life of the sea and that of the fields are too closely linked. But there has always been plenty of fishing and, in times of trouble, it has always been easy to recruit crews for privateers in the overpopulated island. The Ibiza privateers had their days of glory in the 18th century when they chased the Berbers and the English across the Mediterranean.

Meanwhile, the island had to defend itself against pirates; from the Middle Ages, the Moors came periodically to raid the coasts. Watch-towers were built at the top of the cliffs; the town of Ibiza was protected by an imposing citadel where the people sheltered in times of danger. In the interior there were no large perched villages such as are found in Majorca or Provence; the villages are, on the contrary, widely dispersed. The centre of resistance was the little church; built on a height (called the "Puig de la Missa") the church of Ibiza was also a stronghold with blind walls and battlements, a shelter which could hold all the parishioners; it contained a cistern, communal wheat store places, and fortified shops which maintained close links with the rural communities.

But Ibiza's greatest wealth is salt. The salt marshes are at the southern point of the island and have always constituted its main resource. Not that there was any lack of salt in the Mediterranean, but the "red salt" of Ibiza was particularly valued, especially as it had the advantage of being easily accessible at a junction of sea routes, where foreign ships could call. In the Middle Ages, Ibiza really developed a "civilization of salt". The salt marshes were exploited on behalf of great Italian companies which exported salt in all directions and particularly to Northern Italy. The island people were chiefly employed in this work and many foreign workers were brought in (it was said that the Genoese sent Eastern slaves to "work the salt" on Ibiza; Moorish prisoners were certainly used in the salt mines). A point was reached at which essential produce was neglected and it was forbidden to deliver salt to any ship that did not bring grain into the harbour. Subsequently the northern people came who had not enough French salt from Bourgneuf or Portuguese salt from Setubal to salt their herring and their cod. Dutch ships which brought German wheat to the Mediterranean, called at Ibiza on their way back; later came the Norwegian trawlers on their return from fishing expeditions.

IBIZA-TOWN

The capital of the island—also called Ibiza—has 15,000 inhabitants. Perched on a hill, the town dominates a well-sheltered harbour. Seen from the sea, Ibiza has a very decided Oriental, even African appearance, with its jumble of white houses on the slope leading up to the citadel. There is still some activity in the harbour owing to the coastal traffic with the other islands and the salt trade.

Like most Mediterranean fortified towns, Ibiza has an upper town enclosed by a wall and a "marina", the part near the harbour used by the sailors and fishermen where we now find modern shops and hotels. A little way out, towards the E, is another district called the Peña, of medieval origin, where the small shopkeepers, artisans and immigrants used to live; it is a very picturesque and cosmopolitan district, with low houses with terraces and narrow streets broken by archways.

The **Upper Town** was an Arab fortress—as at Palma—where the Palace, the *Almudaina* stood. The present town wall is relatively modern; it was built by Philip II who wanted to make Ibiza one of Spain's main bases in the Mediterranean (a considerable number of the ships for the Armada were concentrated here).

Coming from the harbour, a sloping street goes through the outer wall at the *Puerta de las Tallas* which used to be defended by a draw-bridge; above the gate is the coat-of-arms of King Philip II and two Roman statues. From there we have to go up to the top of the hill where there is an esplanade, now *Plaza de la Catedral* the finest *ensemble* in the town, in the midst of an aristocratic district of churches and convents. From a *terrace* (the Mirador d'Ibiza) we overlook the sea to the south and have a fine view of the town, the harbour and the outskirts.

The **Cathedral** was built on the site of a former mosque shortly after the reconquest. Unfortunately it was mostly destroyed and was rebuilt in the 18th century in a rather heavy baroque style; of the 13th century only the finely proportioned square belfry remains and, in the interior, some statues (by *Adrien Ferran*, the Virgin of the altar) and altar-pieces. Very fine *panorama* from the top of the tower, and from a terrace which we reach by a little street running along the south side of the church (view of the harbour and the coast).

In the cathedral square we can see on one side the ruins of the old Almudaina dominated by the *Tower of Homage* and the episcopal palace, on the other the old *Town Hall* which now houses the **Archaeological Museum;** a visit to it is essential to an understanding of the old civilizations of the island (other items found during excavations on Ibiza are also in the Archaeology Museum in Madrid); the Phoenician and Punic series comprise a quantity of coins, terra-cotta statuettes of Oriental make, and all kinds of implements.

From the cathedral we can go back down to the Town Hall which occupies a part of the old *Dominican Friary* (note particularly two 15th-century cloisters). The church of this monastery, *San Domingo*, still survives though it was completely rebuilt in the 18th century: baroque façade and rich decoration in the interior.

From the other side of the hill, to the W, we leave the cathedral square by a series of very steep picturesque little streets: houses with casement windows in stone and characteristic balconies, little chapels, arched passages. Thus we come to the **New Gate,** the main bastion of the walls, of very unusual design.

Beyond the town walls a path leads in about 10 minutes to the *necropolis* of *Ereso*, also known as the necropolis of the *Puig dels Molins* because several windmills were built there to grind the corn from the island of Formentera. There are more than 2,000 graves some of which—of considerable size—contain sarcophagi and utensils; they all date from the Carthaginian period (Ibiza was occupied by the Phoenicians and Carthaginians towards the middle of the 7th century B.C.).

The **district of Peña,** E of the harbour, is very different from the Upper Town; no remarkable buildings but a labyrinth of tiny, busy streets, lines with low serried houses. In the course of haphazard trips through this part—for here we must explore as the fancy takes us—we shall come across unexpected sights and sometimes fine views of the harbour. The busiest spot is the little square where the women get water from the fountain.

The **Marina** near the harbour, however, is modern with pleasant wide promenades: the *Paseo Vara del Rey*, the busiest street, is named after the Spanish general who distinguished himself in Cuba at the end of last century during the Spanish-American war; his statue stands on the avenue.

At the start of the Paseo, note the *Ethnographic Museum* which has interesting collections illustrating the life of the island's people: costumes, furniture, jewels, weapons, and tools. Near the harbour is the Church of the Sailors *(Church of San Telmo)*, an old fortified building with a sober façade; following a tradition, the women go to Sunday Mass there dressed in their ceremonial costume, wearing all their jewels, and especially their heavy gold necklaces. At the foot of the slope leading to the Upper Town: *Plaza del Mercado* with a picturesque fish-market.

Excursions in the island

The tourist who has spent a day seeing the town should devote another day to seeing the island; all the roads converge towards the capital; they are few, but they enable us to see the strange villages and the pleasant and varied countryside. In the country a Catalan dialect is spoken (the island was colonized after the reconquest as is testified by all the villages named after saints) and customs have often remained very characteristic.

1. San José (14 km. from Ibiza by a little country road, to the W). Baroque *church* not very noteworthy; but a path leads to the seashore, to a deep inlet (the *Cala d'Hort*) from where we have a fine view of the remarkable *islet of the Vedra;* this is an immense rock which rises steeply to a height of over 1,310 feet. From San José we can also climb the *Atalayasa*, the highest peak on the island (1,558 feet).

2. The salt works: take the little road to San José as before; at 2 km. on the left a road leads to *San Jorge* (typical fortified church) and thence to the main salt works of Ibiza.

3. San Juan Bautista; 22 km. N. Follow the island's main road; after 2 km. a small road to the right goes to *San Jesus* (church with strange Gothic altar-piece).

After 6 km., on the left, the road to *San Gertrudis* and *San Miguel* (16 km. from Ibiza). These two typical villages each have a very noteworthy church: that of San Gertrudis is the typical fortified church, very simple with narrow windows and its flat terra-cotta roof. The church of San Miguel (former bishopric) has more stately proportions and a more complex design; in front of it is a vast paved courtyard with wide flagstones, surrounded by arcades where the faithful gathered or where they could entrench themselves.

The road finally comes to *San Juan Bautista*, a pleasant village (baroque church) near the sea which can be reached by narrow paths leading to picturesque inlets; this is the best way of getting to the N coast, the wildest of the island.

4. Santa Eulalia del Río. We can get to this village by a very tiny road which leaves from Ibiza and remains close to the E coast, affording several fine *views* of the cliffs and country (especially near the Puig d'en Valls). But the easiest route is the San Juan road and then a road fork to the right following the smiling, fertile valley of the Río de Santa Eulalia where there are minute *huertas* with orchards and *norias* driven by mules.

Santa Eulalia (21 km. from Ibiza) is a charming village situated at the back of an easy bay; summer residence and very popular bathing resort; the *church* on the top of a hill (the "Puig de la Missa") stands on the site of the former mosque whose porch still survives, an interesting example of Moslem rustic art, giving an impression of solidity, with horseshoe arches at the entrance showing great simplicity of line. The present church—built very late (the old Moorish buildings were being used till the end of the 16th century) is none the less fortified like a stronghold.

This village is becoming increasingly popular as a centre for artists and writers.

5. San Antonio Abad (15 km. from Ibiza by a little road which crosses the island along its whole width). It is a double village; round the *fortified church* dominated by two defence towers, the houses packed close together; near the sea, the *puerto* and its pleasant *beaches*.

6. The islet of Formentera: only 5 km. S of Ibiza, a small island of hardly 100 square km.; there is a regular boat service (several times a week) or you can go there in a hired boat. The population (3,000 inhabitants) lives in the port of *Cala Savina* and in the main town, *San Francesco Javier*.

Practical Information

THE
BALEARIC ISLANDS

	Page
Useful addresses in Majorca	103
Useful addresses in Minorca	109
Useful addresses in Ibiza	109
Air services	98
Banks (Palma)	103
Car hire	101
Coaches	101
Communications in Majorca	101
Consulates	103
Customs documents	97
Exchange and Currency	97
Food	98
Hotels	103
Museums	106
Passports	97
Post and Telegraph Offices	106
Railways	101
Restaurants	100
Sea (connexions by)	99
Seasons	97
Shows	106
Sports	106
Tourist information	97
Traditional festivals	97
Travel agencies	103
Spanish dictionary	111

I. Planning for the Journey

Enquiries

The Information Centres of the Under-Secretariat of the Spanish Tourism will give any information needed for the trip.

In London:	Spanish National Tourist Office, 70 Jermin Street, tel. 930 8578.
In New York:	5th Avenue 189, New York 10017, tel. 759 3842.
In Toronto:	13 Queen Street East, tel. Empire 4–2125.
In Geneva:	1 Rue de Berne, tel. 31 69 40.
In Palma:	Subsecretaria de Turismo, Avda Jaime III 56, tel. 12216.
In Madrid:	Subsecretaria de Turismo, Avda Medinaceli 2, tel. 2222830.
In Ibiza:	Subsecretaria de Turismo, Vara del Rey, 13, tel. 191.

Passports and customs documents

Tourists going to Spain need a valid passport. Visas are not required for Canadian, British or American citizens.

A carnet de passage or Triptych is no longer required. An international driving licence is also required. These documents in England may be obtained from Tourist associations (Automobile Association or Royal Automobile Club). Motorists also must have the green Insurance Card which is issued by their Insurance Companies.

Exchange and Currency

The Spanish monetary unit is the peseta (pta) divided into 100 centimos. The present rate of exchange is approximately $ 1.43 for 100 pesetas. The tourist leaving Spain is allowed to take only 9,000 ptas out of the country.

Seasons

A stay in the Balearic Islands is pleasant at any time of year. In the summer the islands attract chiefly beach and boating enthusiasts; the winters are renowned for their mildness. Spring and autumn are sometimes wet, but not in any regular way.

The chief *traditional festivals* are:

17 Jan. at Manacor: feast and procession of San Anton.
20 Jan. at Pollensa: feasts of San Sebastien; folk-dancing.
3 May at Selva: feast of Santa Crux; dancing and processions.
26 July at Valldemosa: feasts of Santa Catalina Thomàs.

1st Sunday in August at Palma: Cavalcade in honour of Santa Catalina Thomàs.
2 August at Pollensa: feasts of the "Moros y Christianos".
8 September at Mahon (Minorca): feast of Nuestra Señora de Gracia; processions.
Holy Week celebrations in Palma are of special interest.

Meals and cuisine

As elsewhere in Spain mealtimes are much later than in France or England. The usual times are 2 to 3 p.m. and towards 10 p.m. In Palma, however, since the growth of tourism and the influx of so many foreigners, it is possible to have meals served considerably earlier if one wishes.

The *cuisine* is often reminiscent of that of Catalonia: specialities are sausage meats (the *sobresada* in particular), paella, fish and sea fruits. Majorca has some very good white wines (Binisalem).

II. Approaches and Communications

By air.

There are several flights daily between Barcelona, Madrid and Palma, Ibiza and Mahon, operated by *Aviaco* and *Iberia*. At Barcelona and Madrid, connexions may be had for New York, (Pan American, Iberia etc.), Toronto *via* New York.

London-Palma:

BEA operates flights from Heathrow Airport to Palma 4 times weekly in the Winter season. Night flights on Saturdays and Sundays. In Summer, several daily connexions. Coach departure is from the West London Air Terminal. Air Terminal in Palma, Avda. Juan March Ordinas 12.

Barcelona-Palma:

Flights operated by Iberia and Aviaco. Daily flights lasting from 30 or 40 mins. (by jet) to 1 hour. Aviaco operates a daily connexion between Palma and Ibiza and between Palma and Mahon. Extra flights in summer.

Addresses of Iberia outside Spain:

Great Britain: London, W.1: 169 Regent Street, tel. GERard 5622.

Glasgow: 45 St. Enoch's Square, tel. City 6581.
Ireland: Dublin: 3 Grafton Arcade, Grafton Street 2, tel. 774368.

Canada: Toronto: 80 Richmond Street W., tel. 363 2612.
U.S.A.: New York: 518 5th Avenue, tel. MU-7-8050.

Addresses of Iberia in Spain:

Palma: Avda. José Antonio 7, tel. 215200.
Barcelona: Rambla de Cataluña 18, tel. 231 6200.
Madrid: Velazquez 130, tel. 261 89 00.

Addresses of BEA in Great Britain and Ireland:

London: Dorland Hall, Low Regent Street S.W. 1, tel. 370-5411.
Glasgow: 122 St. Vincent Street, tel. 332 9666.
Dublin: 38 Westmoreland Street, 77, tel. 772821.

Addresses of BEA in Spain:

Palma: 1 Plaza Pio XII, tel. 214306.
Madrid: Avda. José Antonio 68, tel. 2475300.
Barcelona: Paseo de Gracia 59, tél. 215-2112.

Other addresses:

Pan American World Airways:
  Madrid: Edificio España, Palace Hotel, tel. 241-4200.
  Barcelona: Calle Majorca, 250, tel. 215-2058.

Air France:
  Palma: Plaza Sta Catalina Thomas 35, tel. 215 900

AVIACO:
  Palma: Calle del Conquistador 42, tel. 24104.
  Car-Passenger service from Barcelona to Palma. Transport services by AVIACO. Service operates daily and takes about 1 hour. Fare for cars calculated on length.

By sea.

1. Regular services are assured by the *Trasmediterránea Cie.* from ports on the Peninsula, as follows:

  Barcelona–Palma: daily. Departure 24 hrs, arriving 8 a.m. Every day except Thursday and

	Sunday: departure 12 hrs., arrival 8 p.m.
Palma–Barcelona:	same timetable and frequencies.
Barcelona–Mahon:	1 connexion daily except on Saturdays and Sundays. Duration: 12 hours. Night trip.
Mahon–Barcelona:	1 connexion daily except sn Sundays and Mondays.
Barcelona–Ibiza:	4 connexions weekly in both directions Duration 12 hours.
Valencia–Palma:	4 weekly connexions. The trip takes II hours.
Valencia–Ibiza:	2 services in each direction weekly. The trip tales 12 hours.

Services between Palma and the other islands operated by the Trasmediterránea:

Palma–Mahon return: One weekly connexion in each direction. The trip takes II hours.

Palma–Ibiza return: 3 weekly connexions lasting 7 hours.

There are more frequent connexions in the summer. There are also regular services between Alicante and Palma or Ibiza, and between Palma and Ciudadela.

Fares for these crossings are approximately as follows;

	1st class	2nd class	3rd class
Barcelona–Palma	1043 pesetas	560	–
Valencia–Palma	655 pesetas	420	310
Palma–Mahon	467 pesetas	239	162

Prices are lower in the off-season.

For car transport (cars are taken on all ships; booking necessary): a car weighing 1000 kg. and 5 metres long costs approximately 1,200 pesetas for shipment from Barcelona to Palma.

Addresses of the *Trasmediterránea*:

Palma: Muelle (on the Port), tel. 22 67 40.

PRACTICAL INFORMATION

Barcelona: Via Layetana, 2, tel. 21 996 12.
Valencia: Paz, 29, tel. 21 72 10.
Alicante: Esplanada de España, 3, tel. 21 18 52.

2. The *Cie de Navigation Mixte* runs regular services in summer between Marseille–Algiers, calling at Palma (once a week).
Addresses of the Company:
Paris: 1, Rue Scribe.
Marseille: 1, La Canebière.
Palma: Agencia Schembri, Avenida A. Maura.
Algiers: 2, Boulevard de la République.

3. The *Zim Israel Navigation Company* runs a service New York–Palma–Naples–Haifa ((about once every 20 days).
Addresses:
Barcelona: Via Layetana 5.
Palma: Paseo del Generalisimo 39.

Communications in Majorca:

Private cars:

Private cars may be shipped (reserve shipping space beforehand) from Barcelona, Valencia or Alicante.
It is easy to hire self-drive cars (Fiat, Renault, SEAT).

Addresses:

Atesa: Plaza de Pio XII, 8, tel. 22 53 47.
Avis: Monseñor Palmer, tel. 23 36 94.
Autos Cort: General Goded, 41, tel. 21 50 91.
Garage Enseñat: Padre Bartolomé Pou, 110, tel. 25 08 54.
Hertz: Paseo Marítimo (edificio Mar), tel. 23 48 33.
Meliá: Paseo del Generalísimo, 74, tel. 21 40 06.
Moto-Sport: Héroes de Manacor, 76–78, tel. 21 53 21.

Trains

Several services daily on all the lines in the island (from Palma to Santañy, Felanitx, Artà, La Puebla, Manacor, Inca, Soller).
Railway Travel Office: Plaza España, Tel. 25 22 45.

Motor coaches

Regular services, at least once a day, to all the towns in Majorca. Departures, according to direction, from:

Railway Station (NE and E).
Avenida Alejandro Rossello 31 (SE).
Calle 31 de Diciembre (North)
Via Roma 4 (SW).

Organized excursions

The main travel agencies (see addresses below, p. 103) or transport companies organize coach excursions to the most interesting places on the island. Tickets from the travel agencies or hotels. Generally excursions take place on the following days (in Summer).

Monday and Thursday: Valldemosa, Mirama, Soller, Puerto de Soller, Raxa gardens.

Wednesday and Sunday: Manacor, Caves of Hams and Drach, Porto Cristo.

Tuesday, Friday and Sunday: Formentor and Puerto de Pollensa.

Tuesday and Saturday: Lluch, La Calobra, Torrent de Pareys.

Tuesday and Saturday: morning: sightseeing tour of Palma (on foot). Afternoon: tour of the surroundings of Palma by coach.

Saturday: Canyamel and visit to the Caves of Artà.

Saturday: Camp de Mar (beach).

Palma city bus services

Main Lines in services:

1 Plaza del Mercado–Lareal–Establiments.
3 Plaza de la Reina–Terreno–Porto Pi.
4 Plaza de la Reina–Ca's Catala.
5 Plaza de la Reina–Genova.
6 Plaza Pio XII–Porto Pi.
8 Plaza Pio XII–Son Roca.
9 Puerta de S. Antonio–Son Dureta
10 Puerta de S. Antonio–Son Espanyolet.
12 Avda A. Rosseló–Pont d'Inca.
14 Avda A. Rosseló–C'an Pastilla
15 Plaza de S. Antonio–La Soledad.
17 Circunvalación (Circular line).
19 Plaza del Olivar–Coliseo (Plaza de Toros).
24 Avda A. Rosseló–Aeropuerto.

III. Useful Addresses

MAJORCA

Palma

1. TRAVEL AGENCIES

   Baixas, Soledad 16, Tel. 22 52 54.
   Cía. Hispanoamericana de Turismo, Paseo Generalisimo, Tel. 21 74 60.
   España Mundial, José Tous Ferrer 21, Tel. 22 26 64.
   FRAM, Arabi, Tel. 22 21 46.
   Iberia, Paseo Generalisimo 48, Tel. 22 67 43.
   I.C.A.B., Pelaires 103, Tel. 21 49 60.
   Internacional Expreso, General Goded 37, Tel. 22 30 30.
   Meliá, Generalisimo 57, Tel. 21 40 05.
   Ultramar Express, Av. Jaime III, Tel. 22 70 45.
   Wagons-Lits Cook, Paseo Generalisimo 57, Tel. 22 21 29.

2. BANKS

   Banco de Bilbao, Plaza Virgen de la Salud, 1, Tel. 21 54 00.
   Banco de España, San Bartolomè 40
   Banco Hispano Americano, Sindicate 10, Tel. 22 46 03.
   Banco de Santander, Jaime II 38–40, Tel. 22 26 57.

3. CONSULATES

   Argentina: Avenida Alejandro Rossello 40, Tel. 21 21 60.
   Belgium: Santo Domingo 22, Tel. 21 22 21.
   Brazil: Balmes 57, Tel. 21 55 31.
   Colombia: Piedad 15, Tel. 21 71 52.
   Costa-Rica: Miramar 26, Tel. 21 21 39.
   Chile: Via Roma 57, Tel. 21 22 79.
   Netherlands: Avda, Antonio Maura 64, Tel. 21 53 05.
   France: General Mola 43, Tel. 22 41 00.
   Great Britain: General Mola, 6, Tel. 21 20 85.
   Greece: Marquès de la Cenia 59, Tel. 21 39 92.
   Italy: Alm. Oquendo 32, Tel. 23 92 05
   Portugal: Salud, 1, Tel. 23 04 24.
   Sweden: General Mola, 6, Tel. 22 54 92.

HOTELS

Luxury Class

   at Terreno, near the sea:
   Bahia Palace, Fénix, Mediterraneo Gran Hotel, Son Vida.

at Ca's Catalá: Maricel.
at Calamayor: Nixe Palace (beach).

1st Class

in town:
Residencia Alhambra, Avda Antonio Maura, 36.
Capitol, Plaza del Rosario.
Catalonia, Massanet, 3.
Colon, Calle 31 de Diciembre.
Jaime I, Paseo Mallorca, 2.
Palma, Plaza Garcia Orell, 14.
Regina, San Miguel, 189.

at Terreno, near the sea:
Augusta, Dux, Rigel, Victoria, Costa Azul, Embajador, Mirador, Miramar, Virginia.
at Ca's Català: Villa Montserrat.
at Calamayor: Calamayor, La Cala, Panoramico, Bristol, Santa Ana, Vistamar.

2nd class

in town:
Balear, Plaza Mayor.
Comercio, José Tous Ferrer, 4.
Londres, Gran Via José Antonio, 2.
San Luis, Veri 11.

at Terreno, near the sea:
Hidalgo, Marfil, Voramar.
At Calamayor: Bella Costa.

3rd class

in town:
Buenos Aires, Conde Sallent, 109.
Perù, Palou y Coll, 18.
San Cayetano, via San Cayetano, 15.
at Terreno, near the sea:
Ciudad Jardin, Eden Roc, Vista Alegre, York.
at Calamayor: Los Leones, Gales.

5. BOARDING HOUSES

As everywhere in Spain, there are very many boarding houses in Palma. They usually are in private houses and mostly are extremely comfortable and pleasant to stay in. Below is a selection only of addresses.

Luxury Class:

in town: Bell-Pi, Calle Mas 4.
near the sea: Almirante, Americana (apartments), Emperatriz, Pergola, Rocamar, Villa Nova.
at Calamayor: Chipre, Acor, Almirante, Cala Nova.

1st class

in town:
Hostal de la Almoyna, Capiscolato, 2.
Bosch, Jaime Ferrer, 12.
Internacional, Olmos, 166.
Olivar, San Miguel, 89.
near the sea: numerous boarding houses in the Terreno district, especially at the seaside; particularly in Calle Calvo Sotelo.
at Ca's Català: Ca's Català, Montserrat.
at Calamayor: Goyena, Rimini.
at Ca'n Pastilla: Oasis.

2nd class: mainly in the centre and the northern and eastern suburbs;

only a very few at the seaside.

6. HOTELS AND BOARDING HOUSES *in the surroundings of Palma.*

on the west coast

at Illetas (10km.): Illetas (1st class), Bonsol (1st class).
at Palma Nova (14 km.): Morocco, Playa Palma Nova, Pinos Mar (1st class).
at Portals Nous (10 km.): Pension Los Pinos (1st class).
at Bendinat (10 km.): Hotel Bendinat (1st class).

on the east coast

at la Playa de El Arenal (10 km.). 1st class: Hotels Acapulco, Copacabana, Leman, Lido, Maritimo, Neptuno; Pensions, Bella Playa, Brisas, Condor, Montemar, Tivoli.
2nd *class*: Hotels Los Angeles, Biarritz, pensions Las Gaviotas, Villa Sol.

7. POST OFFICES

Gran Via José Antonio 6, tel. 21 12 21.
and at Terreno: Calvo Sotelo.
Telephone: Gran Via José Antonio 2, tel. 004.

8. RESTAURANTS

Antonio, Paseo Generalisimo, 21, tel. 22 26 13.
Bellver, Plaza Gomila, tel. 23 00 16.
Cantàbrico, Calvo Sotelo, 304, tel. 23 20 12.
El Faro, Paseo de Sagrera, 7, tel. 22 62 12.
El Patio, Schembri, 5, tel. 23 24 41.
Oriente, Paseo Generalisimo, 80, tel. 22 60 18.
Triton, Calle Estanco, tel. 21 77 84.

9. MUSEUMS, SHOWS AND SPORTS.

Municipal Museum (Bellver Castle). Archaeology. 9.30 a.m.–1.30 p.m. and 5.30 p.m. to sunset; admission 16 ptas; 6 ptas on Sunday.

Provincial Museum (Lonja). Paintings. 10 a.m.–12 noon and 3–5 p.m.; admission 2 ptas.

Episcopal Museum: Archaeology, sculptures, paintings, ceramics. 10 a.m.–1 p.m. and 4–6 p.m. admission 5 ptas.

Cathedral Treasury. 10.30 am.–1 p.m. and 4–7.30 p.m. admission 15 ptas.

Maritime Museum (Consulado de Mar). Ships, weapons, maps; 9 a.m.–1 p.m. and 4–7 p.m.; admission 10 ptas.

Biblioteca Pública Provincial, C. Lulio 10–13.

Museo Krekovic at Son Fuesteret. Open from April 1 to November 1 from 11 a.m. to 1 p.m. and from 6 p.m. to 9 p.m.. Admission 15 ptas.

Theatres:

Balear, calle Zanoguera.
Lirico, Plaza Libertad.
Principal, Plaza Weyler.

Cinemas:

Astoria, Navarra. 13.
Augusta, Conde Sallent, 2.
Avenida, Avda Alejandro.
Born, Paseo Generalisimo, 31.
Rialto, San Felio, 9.

Cabarets:

Aquarium, Paseo Maritimo.
Casablanca, Plaza Lonja, 9.
Saint Tropez, Paseo Maritimo.
Trocadero, via Roma, 1.
and in several hotels in Terreno.

Sports:

Bull fights.
Fronton Baléar.
Real Tennis Club.
Boating Club.

OTHER TOWNS

Alcudia

at *Puerto de Alcudia:* Golf Hotel (1st class), Mar y Sol, Club Carabella.
Miramar (3rd class); pension Ca'n Fumat (1st class).
at *Mal Pas:* Pensions Mal Pas (1st class), Mariposa (2nd class).

Andraitx

at *Puerto de Andraitx:* Hotels Brismar, Villa Italia (1st class); Pensions El Faro, Moderno (1st class).
at *Camp de Mar:* Hotels Camp de Mar, Villa Real (1st class), Playa (2nd class).

Bañalbufar

Hotel Camp de Mar, Marivent (3rd class); Pension Baronia (2nd class).

La Calobra

Pension Hostal La Calobra (luxury).

Capdepera, on the beach:

at *Cala Ratjada:* Hotels Castillo, Son Moll, Bella Playa (1st class); Pensions Ca's Bombu, El Cortijo (1st class), Miramar (2nd class).

at *Canyamel:* Hotel Cuevas (1st class).

Calvià, on the beach:

at *Cala Fornells:* Hotel Cala Fornells (2nd class).
at *Magaluf:* Hotel Atlantic (1st class), Flamboyan (1st class).
at *Paguera:* Hotels Villamil, Bahia Club (1st class), Bella Colina, La Carabela, Malgrat (2nd class); Pension Hostal.

Playa, Niza, la Noria (1st class), Arcades, Ca'n Tianet, La Concha (2nd class).
at *Santa Ponsa:* Hotel Casablanca (2nd class).

Deyà

Pensions Ca'n Gelat, Hostal d'es Moli (1st class), Miramar, Villa Verde, Ca'n Queet.
at *Lluch-Alcari:* Hotel Costa d'Or (3rd class)

Estellènchs

Pensions Ca'n Manuel, Maristel (2nd class).

Felanitx

Pension Santueri (2nd class).

Formentor

Hotel Formentor (luxury).

Inca

Pension Victoria (2nd class).

Pollensa

at *Cala San Vicente:* Hotels Molins, Cala San Vicente (1st class); Pensions Los Pinos (luxury), Niu (1st class).
at *Puerto de Pollensa:* Hotels Folo, Uyal, Capri, Illa d'Or, Miramar, Pollentia, Sis Pins (1st class), Marina (2nd class); Pensions Els Tamarels (luxury), Luz del Mar, Rex (1st class).

Porto Cristo

Hotels Felip, Perello (3rd class); Pension Porto Cristo (1st class).

Santañy

at *Cala d'Or:* Hotels Cala d'Or, Cala Gran (1st class).
at *Cala Figuera:* Hotel Bona Vista (2nd class).

Soller

Pensions Avenida, Gran Via (1st class), Comercio, Las Golondrinas, Soller (2nd class).
at *Puerto de Soller:* Hotels Eden, Esplèndido (1st class), Costa Brava, Marbella, Mare Nostrum, Marina, Marisol, Miramar, Roma (2nd class); Pensions El Faro, Rosabel (1st class), La Primavera, Posada del Mar (2nd class).

Valldemosa
Pension Hospedaje del Artista (1st class).

USEFUL ADDRESSES IN MINORCA

Mahon
Fomento del Turismo: Calvo Sotelo, tel. 10 13.
Post Office: Calle del Buen Aire.
Telephone: Calvo Sotelo, 4.
Cia. Trasmediterranea: Calle Infantas, 24, tel. 35 10 79.
Aviaco: Calle General Goded, 25.
Iberia Travel Agency: General Goded, 35.
Hotels: Port Mahon (1st class), Bustamanet, Rocamar, Sevilla (3rd class).
Restaurants: Colon, Triton, El Paso.
Cinemas: Salon Alcazar, Actualidades.
Theater: Principal, Victoria.

Ciudadela
Hotel: Eleycon (1st class); Feliciano.
Fondas: Española, Faner.

Fornells
Hotel: Burdo.

USEFUL ADDRESSES IN IBIZA

Ibiza Town
Information Bureau (attached to the Tourist Under-Secretariat): Vara de Rey, 13, tel. 21 19 40.
Post Office: Vara de Rey 7,.
Telegraph: Plaza de Vara de Rey.
Telephone: Calle Antonio Palau.
Trasmediterranea: Conde Rosellon, 5, tel. 31 11 09.
Hotels: Argos, Cenit (1st class), Figueretas, Montesol, Noray (2nd class).

SPANISH DICTIONARY

Current Expressions:

Good day
Good evening
Good night
Good bye
Soon, at once
How are you?
Very well, thank you
Almost
I am ill
I am sorry
What can I offer you?
What do you want?
Do sit down
May I ask a favour of you?
I implore you
Do you understand?
I do not understand
Speak slowly
Tell me
Do you speak English?
I want, would like
Where is this?
What is his name?
Thank you

Expresiones de uso corriente:

Buenos días
Buenas tardes
Buenas noches
Hasta la vista, adios
Hasta luego.
¿Como está usted?
Muy bien, gracias
Tal cual
Estoy indispuesto
Lo siento
¿Qué puedo ofrecerle a usted?
¿Qué quiere usted?
Siéntese, por favor
¿Puedo pedirle un favor?
Se lo ruego
¿Comprende usted?
No entiendo
Hable despacio
Dígame usted
¿Habla usted ingles?
Querría tener...
¿Donde está?
¿Como se llama?
Gracias

The Time

Day
Week
Month
Year
Century
January
February
March
April
May
June
July
August
September

El tiempo

Día
Semana
Mes
Año
Siglo
Enero
Febrero
Marzo
Abril
Mayo
Junio
Julio
Agosto
Septiembre

October	Octubre
November	Noviembre
December	Diciembre
Monday	Lunes
Tuesday	Martes
Wednesday	Miércoles
Thursday	Jueves
Friday	Viernes
Saturday	Sábado
Sunday	Domingo
Today	Hoy
Yesterday	Ayer
To-morrow	Mañana
Day after to-morrow	Pasado mañana
The morning	La mañana
Midday	El medio día
The afternoon	La tarde
The evening	La noche
Midnight	La media noche
An hour	Una hora
Half an hour	Media hora
Quarter of an hour	Un cuarto de hora
A minute	Un minuto
Holiday	Día de fiesta
Work-day	Día de trabajo
New Year's Day	Año nuevo
Palm Sunday	Domingo de Ramos
Holy Week	Semana Santa
Easter	Pascua de Resurrección
Corpus Christi	Corpus Christi
All Saints' Day	Todos los Santos
Christmas	Navidad
End of the Year	Fin de año

At the Restaurant — En el Restaurante

I wish to eat	Deseo comer
The menu	La carta, el menú
The cover charge	El cubierto
Oil	Aceite
Butter	Mantequilla
Roast, grill	Asado
Game	Caza
Fillet	Filete
Cutlet	Chuletas

Broth, gravy	Caldo
Boiled	Hervido
Cakes	Dulces
The salt cellar	El salero
Salad	Ensalada
Fruit	Frutas
Eggs	Huevos
fried	— fritos
omelette	— en tortilla
Ham	Jamón
Vegetables	Legumbres, Hortalizas
Sausage	Longaniza
Bread	Pan
Fish	Pescado
Pimento	Pimienta
Chicken	Pollo
Cheese	Queso
Sausage (large)	Salchichón
Soup	Sopa
vermicelli	— de fideos
rice	— de arroz
semolina	— de sémola
Truffles	Trufas
Vinegar	Vinagre
Pastries	Pasteles
Dessert	Postre
Tart	Torta
Ice	Helado

Drinks, Coffee — Bebidas, Café

Bring me something to drink	Tráigame algo para beber
Give me a glass of water	Déme un vaso de agua
Lemonade	Limonada
Orangeade	Naranjada
A cup of coffee, with milk	Una taza de café solo, con leche
Beer, small glass of beer, a larger glass of beer	Cerveza, una caña, un doble
Chocolate, Spanish style (thick), French style	Chocolate a la española — a la francesa
Tea	Té
Lemon squash (fresh), orange squash (fresh)	Refresco de limón, de naranja

A bottle of wine, half a bottle of wine	Una botella de vino (media botella de vino)
A glass of wine, a liqueur	Una copa de vino, — — — licor
An aperitif	Un aperitivo
	Unas tapas (aceitunas, patatas fritas)
Waiter, have you a newspaper?	¿Camarero, tiene un periódico?

Shopping / Tienda

Where can I change some money?	¿Dónde puedo cambiar moneda?
Bank	Banco
Interpreter	Intérprete
Guide	Guía
Butcher's Shop	Carnicería
Butter and eggs (shop for)	Mantequería
Fruit and vegetables (shop for)	Frutería
Bakery	Panadería
Optician	Optico
Hairdresser	Peluquero
Perfumery	Perfumería
Tobacconist	Estanco
Book-shop	Librería
Pharmacy-Chemist	Farmacía
Doctor	Médico
Dentist	Dentista
Shoe-shop	Zapatería
Shirt-maker	Camisería
Tailor	Sastre
Clock-maker, Watch-maker	Relojería
Newspaper kiosk	Puesto de periódicos (kiosko)

Hotel / Hotel

A room with single beds	Una habitación con dos camas
A room with a bathroom	Una habitación con baño
A room facing the street	Habitación con ventana a la calle
Overlooking the courtyard (patio)	Con vistas al patio
How much is it please, with service included?	¿Cuanto cuesta, servicio incluído?

How much is full board (pension) (what are the "en pension" terms)?	¿Cuanto la pensión completa?
I would like another blanket or eiderdown	Quisiera una manta más
I shall be leaving to-morrow afternoon	Me marcho mañana por la tarde
I must leave to-day	Es necesario que salga hoy
Please call me at 8 a.m.	Haga el favor de llamarme a las ocho
May I have the bill?	Prepáreme la cuenta
The waiter	El camarero
The chambermaid	La doncella
Please bring me breakfast at 9 a.m.	Entreme el desayuno a las nueve
A jug of water	Una jarra de agua
Where is the bathroom (the W.C.)?	¿Dónde está el cuarto de baño? (o las retretes)
Breakfast	El desayuno
Lunch	El almuerzo
The Meal	La comida
Dinner	La cena
I have some dirty laundry	Tengo ropa para lavar
Would you post these letters for me?	¿Quiere echarme estas cartas al correo?
Is there any mail for me?	¿Hay alguna carta para mi?
May I have some writing paper?	¿Tiene papel de cartas?

Post

Correos

Where is the Main Post Office, the nearest Post Office?	¿Donde está la casa de Correos? — — la estafeta más próxima?
May I have a stamp for...?	Déme un sello de...
Post-card	Una tarjeta postal
Poste Restante	Lista de correos
Postal transfer (money)	Giro postal
Telegraphic transfer	Giro telegráfico
I would like to send a telegram	Quisiera enviar un telegrama
How much does each word cost?	¿Cuanto cuesta cada palabra?
Reply paid	Respuesta pagada
Urgent	Urgente
Letter-box	Buzón
How much is the postage?	¿Cuanto cuesta el franqueo?

Railway

	Ferrocarril
Time-table or Indicator	Guía de ferrocarriles
First class to...	Un billete de primera clase para...
Return	Ida y vuelta
How much does the ticket cost?	¿Cuanto vale el billete?
When does the train leave?	¿Cuando sale el tren?
Where is the Waiting Room?	¿Dónde está la sala de espera?
Is the train late?	¿Viene el tren con retraso?
Is this the train for...?	¿Es éste el tren de...?
Where does one register luggage?	¿Dónde se facturan los equipajes?
Where can one get a packed lunch?	¿Dónde podría comprar una bolsa de merienda?
The Restaurant car	El coche-restaurante
The Sleeper	El coche-cama
Pillow	Almohada de viaje
Left luggage office	Depósito de equipajes
Porter	El mozo de estación
Place Reservations	Reserva de asiento
Is this seat (place) free?	¿Está libre este asiento?

Customs — Aduana

Nothing to declare	Nada que declarar
I have only my personal belongings with me	Sólo llevo efectos personales
No tobacco	Tabaco, no
No liqueurs	Licores, no
Bags, parcels	Maletas, paquetes
Here are the keys	Aquí están las llaves
The Passport	El pasaporte
Triptych (Carnet for cars)	El triptico

Motor Cars — Automóviles

Vehicle	Coche
Petrol Station	Depósito de gasolina
Petrol (special)	Plomo
Oil	Aceite
Carburettor	Carburador
Front wheel, rear wheel	Rueda delantera, trasera
The horn	El claxón
The starter	El contacto
Mudguard	Guardabarros
Coachwork (chassis)	Carrocería

Engine	Motor
Steering wheel	Volante
Brake	Freno
Headlight	Faro
Garage	Garaje
Petrol Station	Surtidor de gasolina
Service Station	Estación de engrase
Spare parts	Piezas de recambio
Parking authorized	Sitios de estacionamiento
To park	Aparcar
Registration number	Matrícula
The tryes need air	Los neumáticos necesitan presión
The engine has seized	El motor está agarrotado
The car has broken down	Tengo una avería

On the road — En la carretera

Where does this road lead to please?	¿A dónde va esta carretera?
Which is the nearest village?	¿Cual es el pueblo más próximo?
Which is the shortest route to...?	¿Cual es el camino más corto para llegar a...?
What is the name of the nearest village?	¿Cómo se llama el primer pueblo?
What is the state of the road?	¿En qué estado está la carretera?
Keep to the right	Se circula por la derecha
The bridge	El puente
The river	El río
The mountain	La montaña
Where can we find accommodation?	¿En qué sitio podremos encontrar alojamiento?
How long does it take to get to...?	¿Cuanto tiempo se necesita para ir a...?
The pass (defile or gorge)	El puerto
The ascent	La subida
The descent	La bajada
The speed	Velocidad
Road barred	Prohibido el paso
Warning	Atención
The height	La altura

INDEX

I. MAJORCA 22

Alaro 63
Albufadia 61
Albufera (la) 67
Alcudia 66
Algaida 69
Andraitx 54
Arenal (El) 51
Arta 72, 73

Bañalbufar 55
Barranch 60
Bellver 48
Bendinat 48
Benem 72
Biniaraix 60
Binisalem 63
Buñola 61
Burguesa (sierra) 53

Calabra (la) 64
Cala Mayor 47
Cala Ratjada 72
Calviá 53
Campanet 68
Campos 74
Capdellá 53
Capdepera 72
Capucorp Vell 74
Ca's Catala 47
Con d'en Rebassa 51

Deyá 59
Drach 71

Els Ham 70
Escapdello 53
Escorca 64
Estellènchs 55

Felanitx 74
Formentor 66

Fornalutx 60
Galilea 54
Genova 50
Granja (la) 56
Gux (pass) 63

Inca 63

La Puebla 68
Lluch 63
Lluchmayor 73

Manacor 69
Miramar 58
Montuiri 69

Palma 29

    Almudaina 31
    Almudaina (calle) 39
    Atarazanas (plaza) 45
    Berga Palace 43
    Borne (El) 30
    Casa Consistorial 35
    Casa Forminguera 38
    Casa Oleo 39
    Casa Oleza 38
    Cathedral 31
    Cayetano 46
    Conquistador (calle) 31
    Consulado de Mar 45
    El Borne 30
    Guadrado (plaza) 36
    Harbour Gate 45
    Jaime II (calle) 43
    Lonja 43
    Maritimo (paseo) 47
    Maura (avenida) 43
    Mayor (plaza) 42
    Merced (church) 42
    Minonas (church) 43
    Mirador Terrace 35
    Montession (church) 37
    Morell Palace 46

Moorish Baths 38
Diocesan Museum 35
Municipal Museum 35
Provincial Museum 45
Palmer Palace 37
Porto Pi 47
Rambla 42
Sagrera (paseo) 43
Santa Catalina 47
S. Catalina Tomas 43
S. Clara 37
S. Cruz 45
S. Eulalia 35
S. Felipe Neri 42
S. Francisco 36
S. Jeronimo 37
S. Lorenzo 45
S. Miguel 42
S. Nicolas 43
Sollerich Palace 46
Templo (plaza) 37
Terreno 30, 47
Vivot Palace 36
Weyler (plaza) 43

Palma Nova 48
Pareys 61
Pollensa 65
Porreras 75
Porto Cristo 71
Puebla (la) 68
Puerto de Pollensa 66
Puerto de Soller 60
Puerto Colon 75
Puig Mayor 60
Puigpuñent 54

Randa 69
Raxa 62

San Salvador 74
Santa Maria 62
Santa Maria del Puig 65
Santañy 74

Santueri 75
Sarria 56
Soller 59
Son Cigala 54
Son Cleret 50
Son Julia 74
Son Marroig 58
Son Roca 50
Son Zafortezza 54

Torre d'en Beu 74

Valldemosa 56
Villafranca 69

II. MINORCA 77

Addaya 86
Alayor 85
Albufera (la) 82
Alcaufar 82
Algendar 86

Bajoli 85

Caballeria 85
Cala Figuera 82
Cala Mezquida 82
Calas Covás 83
Castells 85
Ciudadela 83

Fornels 85

Gaumès 85

Llafuda (torre) 86

Mahon 78
Mercadal 85
Monte Toro 85

Naveta Els Tudons 84

Pregonda 86

San Antonio 77
San Clemente 83

Sanicera 85
San Luis 82
Talati de Dalt 85
Talayot of Torello 82
Torrauba 85
Villa Carlos 82

III. IBIZA 87

Atalayasa 93
Cala d'Hort 93
Formentera 89

Ibiza-Town 90
  Almudaina 91
  Cathedral 91
  Ereso 92
  Marina 93
  Mirador 91
  Museums 92, 93
  New Gate 92
  Pases Vara del Rey 93
  Peña 92
  Puerta de las Tallas 91
  Puig dels Molins 92
  San Domingo 92
  San Telmo 93
  Tower of Homage 91
  Town Hall 92
  Upper Town 91

Isla of the Vedra 93
Salt works of Ibiza 92
San Antonio Abad 93
San Gertrudis 93
San Jesus 93
San Jorge 93
San José 93
San Juan Bautista 93
San Miguel 93
Santa Eulalia del Río 93

Printed in Switzerland

NOTES

NOTES

NOTES

NOTES

NOTES

This guide has been set, printed and bound by Nagel Publishers
in Geneva (Switzerland)
Legal Deposit Nr. 306
Printed in Switzerland